From Nuremberg to The Hague
The Future of International Criminal Justice

This collection of essays is based on a lecture series organised jointly by the Wiener Library, Matrix Chambers and University College London's Centre for International Courts and Tribunals between April and June 2002. The series was sponsored by the *Guardian* newspaper. Presented by leading experts in the field, this fascinating collection of papers examines the evolution of international criminal justice from its post-Second World War origins at Nuremberg through to the concrete proliferation of courts and tribunals with international criminal law jurisdictions based at The Hague and Arusha. Original and provocative, the lectures provide various stimulating perspectives on the subject of international criminal law. Topics include its corporate and historical dimension as well a discussion of the Statute of the International Criminal Court and the role of national courts, and offers a challenging insight into the future of international criminal justice. This is an intelligent and thought-provoking book, accessible to anyone interested in international justice, from specialists to non-specialists alike.

PHILIPPE SANDS is Professor of Laws and Director of PICT's Centre for International Courts and Tribunals at University College London, and a practising barrister at Matrix Chambers. Contributors include Cherie Booth QC, Andrew Clapham, James Crawford SC, Richard Overy and Philippe Sands.

From Nuremberg to The Hague

The Future of International Criminal Justice

Edited by

PHILIPPE SANDS
University College London

PUBLISHED BY THE PRESS SYNDICATE OF THE UNIVERSITY OF CAMBRIDGE
The Pitt Building, Trumpington Street, Cambridge CB2 1RP, United Kingdom

CAMBRIDGE UNIVERSITY PRESS
The Edinburgh Building, Cambridge CB2 2RU, UK
40 West 20th Street, New York, NY 10011–4211, USA
477 Williamstown Road, Port Melbourne, VIC 3207, Australia
Ruiz de Alarcón 13, 28014 Madrid, Spain
Dock House, The Waterfront, Cape Town 8001, South Africa

http://www.cambridge.org

First published 2003
Reprinted 2004

Printed in the United Kingdom at the University Press, Cambridge

Typeface Minion (*Adobe*) 11/16pt   *System* QuarkXPress®   [PND]

A catalogue record for this book is available from the British Library

ISBN 0 521 82991 7 hardback
ISBN 0 521 53676 6 paperback

Contents

Notes on the contributors

CHERIE BOOTH is a graduate of the London School of Economics, and was called to the Bar in 1976 and took silk in 1995. A member of Matrix Chambers in London, Ms Booth practises principally in the areas of employment and discrimination law, which involves regular advice to clients on the implications of the Human Rights Act. She has appeared before the European Court of Justice and in Commonwealth jurisdictions, and has sat as an international arbitrator. She also sits as a Recorder in the County Court and Crown Court. Ms Booth lectures widely on human rights law. She is a bencher of the Lincoln's Inn and an honorary bencher of the King's Inns. Ms Booth is also Chancellor of Liverpool John Moores University.

ANDREW CLAPHAM is Professor of Public International Law at the Graduate Institute of International Studies in Geneva. He has taught international human rights law and public international law at the Institute since 1997. He served as legal adviser and representative of the Solomon Islands at the 1998 Rome Inter-Governmental Conference on an International Criminal Court. Since 2000, he has been the Special Adviser on Corporate Responsibility to the UN High Commissioner for Human Rights, Mary Robinson. Before his appointment at the Institute in Geneva, he was the representative of Amnesty International at the United Nations in New York. He is an associate academic member of Matrix Chambers.

JAMES CRAWFORD SC, FBA is Whewell Professor of International Law and Director of the Lauterpacht Research Centre for International Law, University of Cambridge, as well as a member of Matrix Chambers. He was a Member of the United Nations International Law Commission from 1992 to 2001. During that time, he was responsible for the ILC's Draft Statute for an International Criminal Court (1994), which became the initial negotiating text for the ICC Preparatory Commission. Subsequently, he was Special Rapporteur on State Responsibility (1997–2001). He has written and lectured widely on issues of international criminal law and the ICC. As a member of Matrix Chambers and Gray's Inn, he has a substantial practice as counsel and arbitrator in international courts and tribunals.

RICHARD OVERY is Professor of Modern History at King's College London. He has written extensively on the Third Reich and the Second World War. His books include *Russia's War, Why the Allies Won, Goering* and, most recently, *Interrogations: The Nazi Elite in Allied Hands.* He is currently writing a comparative study of the Hitler and Stalin dictatorships.

PHILIPPE SANDS is Professor of Laws and Director of the Centre for International Courts and Tribunals at University College London. As a practising barrister at Matrix Chambers, he has been involved in some of the leading cases on international criminal law before national and international courts, including the *Pinochet* case in the House of Lords and the *Croatia* v. *Federal Republic of Yugoslavia* case in the International Court of Justice. He served as legal adviser to the Solomon Islands in the negotiation of the Statute of the International Criminal Court.

Preface

On 17 July 1998, a United Nations Diplomatic Conference adopted the Statute for the International Criminal Court. This was the culmination of a process begun at Nuremberg in the aftermath of the Second World War and leading to the creation of a permanent international tribunal which would have jurisdiction over the most serious international crimes.

Three months later, on 16 October 1998, Senator Augusto Ugarte Pinochet, the former President of Chile, was arrested in London pursuant to a request for his extradition to Spain to face charges for crimes against humanity which had occurred while he was head of state in Chile. This marked the first time a former head of state had been arrested in England on such charges, and it was followed by legal proceedings which confirmed that he was not entitled to claim immunity from the jurisdiction of the English courts for crimes which were governed by an applicable international convention.

Seven months later, on 27 May 1999, President Slobodan Milosevic of the Federal Republic of Yugoslavia was indicted by the Prosecutor of the International Criminal Tribunal for the former Yugoslavia for atrocities committed in Kosovo. This marked the first time that a serving head of state had ever been indicted by an international tribunal.

These three developments, taking place in a period of less than a year (and which may or may not be connected), indicated the extent to which the established international legal order was undergoing a transformation, and the emergence of a new system of 'international criminal law'. They were not spontaneous occurrences. Rather, they built on developments in international law over the past fifty years – particularly in the fields of human rights and humanitarian law – which reflect a commitment of the international community to put in place – and to enforce – rules of international law which would bring to an end impunity for the most serious international crimes.

In the summer of 2001, informal discussions at the Wiener Library focused on how to generate greater public awareness of these developments and of their implications, which linked the creation of the International Criminal Court to the epochal trial held at Nuremberg in 1946 (at which leading figures in the

Nazi regime were tried on four counts: of conspiracy, crimes against peace, war crimes and crimes against humanity, as defined in Article 6 of the Charter of the International Military Tribunal). The Wiener Library had been significantly connected to the Nuremberg trials: 'It may be said', a UN Commissioner wrote in November 1946, 'that it is thanks to the Wiener Library that the criminal decrees, regulations, orders and circulars of the Nazi rulers were made known ... The help it has given has been invaluable in the preparation of charges against the leaders of Nazi Germany.' After the trials, Alfred Wiener was offered the papers of the British prosecution team. In 1995, all but one of the last sworn and signed statements of the Nuremberg indictees were donated to the Library.

The Wiener Library then decided that it would be appropriate to broaden its initiative, leading to the involvement of Matrix Chambers and University College London's PICT Centre for International Courts and Tribunals. The result was the series of five public lectures held in London from April to June 2002, organised around the theme 'From Nuremberg to The Hague: The Future of International Criminal Justice'.

The five lectures here published trace the historical and legal developments of international criminal justice in relation to genocide, war crimes and crimes against humanity during the past five decades. They raise a host of questions – political, legal, cultural – on the delivery of international justice, which are of broad public importance and public interest. The five lecturers were invited to address their topics in a manner which would be accessible to the public, and which would trace developments from the Nuremberg proceedings to the establishment of the International Criminal Court, including also the efforts of the international criminal tribunals for Yugoslavia and Rwanda, as well as the role of national courts.

The Statute of the International Criminal Court came into force three weeks after the final lecture, on 2 July 2002. Its judges will be elected in early 2003 and it will begin to function shortly thereafter.

We would like to thank the numerous individuals who contributed to the organisation of these lectures, in particular Noemi Byrd at the PICT Centre and Nick Martin and Anna Edmundson at Matrix Chambers, as well as Alan Rusbridger, Ed Pilkington and Marc Sands at the *Guardian* newspaper for their support for the lecture series. We would also like to thank Max du Plessis and Professor Christine Chinkin for their intellectual contributions, and the distinguished individuals who took time out of their busy schedules to chair individual lectures: David Bean QC, Lord Justice

Stephen Sedley, and Sir Shridath Ramphal QC. We were gratified by the large public turnout at each of the lectures, and by the range of interests represented and questions posed.

Philippe Sands
Professor of Laws, University College London
Barrister, Matrix Chambers

Ben Barkow
Director, Wiener Library

Katharine Klinger
Wiener Library

London, 20 December 2002

1

The Nuremberg trials: international law in the making

RICHARD OVERY

In October 1945, as he awaited trial as a major war criminal, Robert Ley wrote a long and cogent repudiation of the right of the recently victorious Allies to try German leaders for war crimes. The Indictment served on Ley, and others, on 19 October 1945 claimed that '[a]ll the defendants … formulated and executed a common plan or conspiracy to commit Crimes against Humanity as defined'. Ley continued: 'Where is this plan? Show it to me. Where is the protocol or the fact that only those here accused met and said a single word about what the indictment refers to so monstrously? Not a thing of it is true.'[1] A few days later, Ley committed suicide in his cell rather than face the shame of a public trial.

The unease about the legal basis of the trial was not confined to those who were to stand before it. Legal

[1] National Archives II, College Park, Maryland, Jackson main files, RG 238, Box 3, letter from Robert Ley to Dr Pflücker, 24 October 1945, p. 9.

opinion in Britain and the United States was divided on the right of the victors to bring German leaders before a court for war crimes. The Nuremberg Military Tribunal was, as Ley realised, an experiment, almost an improvisation. For the first time the leaders of a major state were to be arraigned by the international community for conspiring to perpetrate, or causing to be perpetrated, a whole series of crimes against peace and against humanity. For all its evident drawbacks, the trial proved to be the foundation of what has now become a permanent feature of modern international justice.

The idea of an international tribunal to try enemy leaders for war crimes arrived very late on the scene. During the war, the Allied powers expected to prosecute conventional war crimes, from the machine-gunning of the survivors of sunken ships to the torture of prisoners-of-war. For this there already existed legal provision and agreed conventions. Yet these did not cover the prosecution of military and civilian leaders for causing war and encouraging atrocity in the first place. Axis elites came to be regarded by the Allies as the chief culprits, men, in Churchill's words, 'whose notorious offences have no special geographical location'.[2] The

---

[2] Public Record Office (=PRO), Kew, London, PREM 4/100/10, note by the Prime Minister, 1 November 1943, p. 2.

greatest difficulty arose over the issue of the treatment of civilians. Enemy generals and admirals might be prosecuted as simple war criminals if the case could be proved that they ordered crimes to be committed. But civilian leaders were different. There was no precedent for judicial proceedings against them (the campaign to 'hang the Kaiser' in 1919 came to naught, and was in any event directed at the supreme military commander, not a civilian head of state).

When the British government began to think about the issue in 1942, the only realistic solution seemed to be to avoid a trial altogether and to subject enemy leaders to a quick despatch before a firing-squad. 'The guilt of such individuals', wrote the Foreign Secretary, Anthony Eden, in 1942, 'is so black that they fall outside and go beyond the scope of any judicial process.'[3] It was Winston Churchill, Britain's wartime prime minister, who arrived at a solution. He revived the old-fashioned idea of the 'outlaw', and proposed that enemy leaders should simply be executed when they were caught. The idea of summary execution (at six hours' notice, following identification of the prisoner by a senior military officer) became the policy of the British government from 1943

[3] PRO, PREM 4/100/10, minute by the Foreign Secretary, 'Treatment of War Criminals', 22 June 1942, pp. 2–3.

until the very end of the war.[4] Five years before, in 1938, outlawry had finally been abolished as a concept in English law by the Administration of Justice Act.

British preference for summary execution was based partly on the genuine, but almost certainly mistaken, belief that public opinion would expect nothing less, and partly on the fear that a Hitler trial would give the dictator the opportunity to use the court case as a rallying point for German nationalism. American lawyers rehearsed a possible Hitler trial, and found to their discomfiture that he would have endless opportunity for making legal mischief, and, at worst, might argue himself out of a conviction. This would make the trial a mockery, and earn the incredulous hostility of public opinion.[5] In America, Churchill won the support of the President, Franklin Roosevelt, and his hardline Treasury Secretary, Henry Morgenthau. But opinion in Washington was divided. The veteran Secretary of War, Henry Stimson, was opposed to summary justice. He favoured a tribunal that reflected Western notions of justice: 'notification to the accused of the charge, the right to be heard, and to

[4] PRO, PREM 4/100/10, note by the Prime Minister, 1 November 1943, pp. 1–4.
[5] NA II, RG 107, McCloy papers, Box 1, Chanler memorandum, 'Can Hitler and the Nazi Leadership be Punished for Their Acts of Lawless Aggression?', n.d. (but November 1944).

call witnesses in his defence.'[6] The War Department believed that it was important for the Allied war effort to demonstrate that democratic notions of justice would be dispensed even for men like Hitler.

The tide was turned from an unusual quarter. In the Soviet Union, jurists insisted that the full penalty could only be imposed on German leaders after there had been a trial. Their experience of the show trials of the 1930s persuaded them that justice had to be popular, visible justice. Soviet spokesmen universally expected German war criminals to be found guilty and executed, as they had expected purge victims to confess their guilt and be shot in the Great Terror. American officials who were keen to avoid the Churchill line latched on to Soviet insistence on the need for a trial, and an unlikely alliance of Communist lawyers and American liberals was mobilised to protest summary justice and to insist on a judicial tribunal. The argument was clinched only by the death of Roosevelt. His successor, Harry Truman, a former small-town judge, was adamant that a trial was both necessary and feasible. When the major powers met in San Francisco in May 1945 to set up the United Nations, the issue was an urgent agenda item. The British

6 NA II, RG 107, Stimson papers, Box 15, Stimson to the President, 9 September 1944, p. 2.

were outmanoeuvred by the American–Soviet alliance and agreement was reached that Axis leaders should be tried by a military tribunal for crimes as yet unspecified. The idea that the trial should be conducted before a military court reflected the prevailing convention that war crimes were a military affair, but in practice the larger part of the subsequent trial was organised and prosecuted by civilian lawyers and judges.

Truman proceeded at once to appoint an American prosecution team under the leadership of the New Deal lawyer Robert H. Jackson, who had cut his teeth on fighting America's powerful industrial corporations in the 1930s under Roosevelt's antitrust legislation.[7] Jackson was the principal architect of the trial and the decisive figure in holding together an unhappy alliance of Soviet, British and French jurists, who represented the only other United Nations states to be allowed to participate in the tribunal. The Soviet prosecution team favoured a trial but treated the proceedings as if the outcome were a foregone conclusion, a show-trial. French lawyers were unhappy with a tribunal whose main basis was to be Anglo-Saxon common law instead of Roman law, and whose procedures were foreign to French legal practice. Above all, the British accepted the

[7]   NA II, RG 107, McCloy papers, President Truman, Executive Order 9547, 2 May 1945.

idea of a trial with great reluctance. They remained sceptical that a proper legal foundation could be found in existing international law, and doubted the capacity of the Allied prosecution teams to provide solid forensic evidence that Axis leaders had indeed committed identifiable war crimes. British leaders were much more squeamish than the Americans about sitting side-by-side with representatives of a Soviet Union whose own responsibility for aggression and human rights violations was popular knowledge. The driving force behind the tribunal was the American prosecution team under Jackson. Without them, an international war crimes tribunal might never have been assembled.

The preparation of the tribunal exposed the extent to which the trial was in effect a 'political act' rather than an exercise in law. When the American prosecution team was appointed in May 1945, there was no clear idea about who the principal war criminals would be, nor a precise idea of what charges they might face. A list of defendants and a list of indictable charges emerged only after months of argument, and in violation of the traditions of justice in all the major Allied powers. The choice of defendants was the product of a great many different strands of political argument, and was not, as had been expected, self-evident. Some of those eventually charged at Nuremberg, like Hitler's former Economics Minister,

Hjalmar Schacht, were given no indication for six months that they might find themselves in the dock. Schacht himself had been taken into Allied custody straight from a Nazi concentration camp.[8]

Quite how arbitrary the choice eventually was can be demonstrated by a remark made by Britain's attorney-general at a meeting in June 1945 to draw up yet another list of defendants: 'The test should be: Do we want the man for making a success of our trial? If yes, we must have him.'[9] The task of assigning responsibility was made more difficult by the death or suicide of the key figures. Hitler killed himself on 30 April 1945; Heinrich Himmler, head of the SS and the managing-director of genocide, killed himself in British custody in May; Joseph Goebbels died with Hitler in the bunker; Benito Mussolini was executed by partisans shortly before the end of the war. This last death accelerated the decision to abandon altogether the idea of putting *Axis* leaders in the dock. Italian names had been included on the early lists of defendants, but by June they had been removed. Italian war criminals were turned over to the Italian government for trial. Italy was now a potential

[8] Imperial War Museum, London, FO 645 Box 154, Foreign Office Research Department, Schacht personality file; PRO, WO 208/3155, Schacht personality file.

[9] PRO, LCO 2/2980, minutes of second meeting of British War Crimes Executive, 21 June 1945, p. 2.

ally of the West. Other Axis allies, like Admiral Horthy of Hungary, were also quietly dropped from the list. By mid-summer all the prosecuting powers had come to accept that they would try only a selection of German political and military leaders.

This decision still begged many questions. In 1945, the international community faced for the very first time the issue of bringing to trial the government of one of its renegade members. In theory the entire governmental and military apparatus could be arraigned: if some were guilty, then, as Robert Ley complained in his tirade against the legal basis of the trial, all were guilty. The early American lists did include a hundred names or more. The British prosecution team, under Sir David Maxwell Fyfe, favoured a smaller and more manageable group, and for much of the summer expected to try only half-a-dozen principal Nazis, including Hermann Göring, the self-styled 'second man in the Reich'. At one point, the British team argued for a single, quick trial using the portly Göring as symbol for the dictatorship.[10] The chief difficulty in drawing up an agreed list of defendants derived from different interpretations of the power-structure of the Third Reich. In 1945, the view was widely held that Hitlerism had been a malign

[10] PRO, LCO 2/2980, minutes of third meeting of British War Crimes Executive, 25 June 1945, pp. 1–4.

extension of the old Prussia of militarism and economic power. The real villains, on this account, were to be found among the Junker aristocracy and the industrial bosses, who were Nazism's alleged paymasters. Clement Attlee, Churchill's deputy prime minister, and then premier himself following Labour's election victory in July 1945, argued forcefully that generals and business leaders should be dragged into the net. 'Officers who behave like gangsters', wrote an uncharacteristically intemperate Attlee, 'should be shot.' He called for a cull of German businessmen 'as an example to the others'.[11]

These views did not go uncontested. The indictment of large numbers of senior officers was regarded as a dangerous precedent, which might allow even the defeated enemy the opportunity to argue that Allied military leaders were just as culpable. The decision to include German bombing as part of the indictment was quietly dropped for just such reasons. The issue of economic criminals was equally tendentious. While Soviet lawyers, British socialists and Jackson's team of New Dealer lawyers saw nothing unjust about including industrial magnates at Nuremberg, they were opposed by those who saw business activity as independent of

[11] PRO, PREM 4/100/10, Deputy Prime Minister, 'Treatment of Major Enemy War Criminals', 26 June 1944.

politics and war-making. Even Albert Speer, Hitler's armaments minister and overlord of the war economy, was argued about. He was, one British official suggested, 'essentially an administrator', not a war criminal.[12] This tendency to see economic leaders as functionaries rather than perpetrators probably saved Speer from hanging when the trial ended in 1946.

The many arguments over whom to indict betrayed a great deal of ignorance and confusion on the Allied side about the nature of the system they were to put on trial. Only gradually over the summer, and thanks to a wealth of intelligence gathering and interrogation, did a clearer picture emerge. But there still remained significant gaps. Knowledge of the extent and character of the Holocaust was limited to information supplied by Jewish organisations. The chief managers of genocide, the Gestapo chief, Heinrich Müller, and his deputy, Adolf Eichmann, were missing from most lists of potential defendants. Because he made more noise than the other party fanatics, the prosecution chose Julius Streicher, editor of the scurrilous anti-semitic journal *Der Stürmer*, as the representative of Nazi racism. Yet Streicher had held no office in the SS racist apparatus, knew nothing of the details of the Holocaust, and had

[12] PRO, LCO 2/2980, British War Crimes Executive meeting, 15 June 1945, p. 2.

lived in disgrace since 1940 after Hitler had sacked him as Gauleiter of Franconia on corruption charges. Full interrogation testimony on the Holocaust and its perpetrators was received only days before the start of the trial in November 1945, when it at last became clear that the men the Allies should have been hunting were still at large.

The final agreed list of twenty-two defendants represented a series of compromises. The original six British names were never in question: Göring, the foreign minister Joachim von Ribbentrop, interior minister Wilhelm Frick, labour front leader Robert Ley, Ernst Kaltenbrunner, head of the security apparatus, and the party's chief ideologue, Alfred Rosenberg. Other names were added as representative of important aspects of the dictatorship. The idea of representation was without question legally dubious, but it resolved many of the disputes between the Allies over how large the eventual trial should be. Streicher stood for anti-semitism; Hitler's military *chef de cabinet*, Wilhelm Keitel, and his deputy for operations, Alfred Jodl, stood for German militarism; the unfortunate Schacht and his successor as economics minister, Walther Funk, were made to represent German capitalism. Jackson insisted that Gustav Krupp, the one industrial name well-known everywhere outside Germany, should also be included, despite his age and his debilitated condition. But he was too ill to attend, and Jackson's efforts to extend the principle of representation by simply requiring Krupp's son, Alfried, to attend in his place was too much for the other prosecution teams, and the trial went ahead with no Prussian 'iron baron' in the courtroom.[13]

Others were included for a variety of reasons. Karl Dönitz, head of the German navy and Hitler's brief successor as chancellor, had his name added at the Potsdam conference, when it was brought up by the Soviet Foreign Minister. Only days before, the British prosecution had warned that the Dönitz case was so weak that he would probably be acquitted, an outcome regarded candidly as 'disastrous to the whole purpose of the trial'.[14] The Soviet Union did not want to be alone in presenting none of its Nazi prisoners at Nuremberg, and in August insisted that Admiral Erich Raeder and an official of Goebbels' propaganda ministry, Hans Fritsche, should also be included. The remaining group of Nazi ministers and officials were deemed to have done

13 On Krupp, see Imperial War Museum, FO 645, Box 152, minutes of meeting of chief prosecutors, 12 November 1945, p. 1. Jackson's views on Krupp are in NA II, RG 238, Box 26, draft of press release.

14 PRO, WO 311/576, British War Crimes Executive to War Office, 20 June 1945; War Office to Supreme Headquarters, Allied Expeditionary Force (Paris), 27 June 1945.

enough to merit their inclusion, but the final list left out men like Otto Thierack, the SS minister of the interior and former head of the Nazi People's Court, and the SS general, Kurt Daluege, head of the Order Police and an important figure in the apparatus of repression and genocide. Both were in Allied captivity. To ensure that even these men would eventually stand trial in a series of subsequent tribunals, the Allied prosecutors, at Jackson's prompting, agreed to arraign a number of organisation as well as individuals. It was hoped that, by declaring the organisations criminal, further trials of individuals now classified as *prima facie* criminals could be speeded up. This was a device of doubtful legality, since it placed much of the basis of war crimes trials on retrospective justice, but nonetheless alongside the twenty-two defendants at Nuremberg stood metaphorically the SS, the SA, the Gestapo and the rest of the German cabinet and military high command.[15]

The framing of the charges was a little less arbitrary. Here there was no precedent at all. The war crimes defined at the end of the First World War and subject to common agreement included crimes that had evidently been perpetrated by the Nazi system: 'systematic terrorism', 'torture of civilians', 'usurpation of sovereignty'

---

[15] NA II, RG 238, Box 34, Indictment first draft, p. 1.

and so on.[16] The difficulty in this case was to define crimes in terms that could be applied to the men in the dock, few of whom could be shown beyond any reasonable doubt to have directly ordered or perpetrated particular crimes, even if they served a criminal regime. The main charge was deemed to be the waging of aggressive war as such, but this had never been defined as a crime in international law, even if its prosecution might give rise to specific criminal acts. War was regarded as legally neutral, in which both sides enjoyed the same rights, even in cases of naked aggression. To define the war-making acts of the Nazi government as crimes required international law to be written backwards. Even more problematic was the hope that the crimes perpetrated against the German people by the dictatorship, and the persecution and extermination of peoples on grounds of race, could also be included in any final indictment. This violated the principle in international law that the internal affairs of a sovereign state were its own business, however unjustly they might be conducted. Here, too, legal innovation was a pre-condition for trial.

The radical solution proposed by Jackson and the American prosecution team was to include all the

---

[16] NA II, RG 107, McCloy papers, Box 1, United Nations War Crimes Commission memorandum, 6 October 1944, Annex A.

actions deemed to be criminal under the single heading of a conspiracy to wage aggressive and criminal war. This tautological device was first thought up in November 1944 by an American military lawyer, Murray Bernays. It had obvious merits beyond that of simplicity. Bernays concluded that a conspiracy to wage aggressive war could rightfully include everything the regime had done since coming to power on 30 January 1933. It could include the deliberate repression of the German people, the plans for rearmament, the persecution of religious and racial minorities, as well as the numerous crimes committed as a consequence of the launching of aggressive war in 1939. Moreover, conspiracy removed the central legal problem that defendants could claim obedience to higher orders in their defence, or that Hitler (who at that point was still alive, and expected to be the chief defendant) could claim immunity as sovereign head of state. Conspiracy caught everyone in the net, regardless of their actual responsibility for specific acts.[17]

The idea of conspiracy remained the essence of the American prosecution case right through to the trial

---

[17] NA II, RG 107, Stimson papers, memorandum on war crimes, 9 October 1944; letter from Stimson to Stettinius (Secretary of State), 27 October 1944, enclosing 'Trial of European War Criminals: The General Problem', pp. 1–5.

itself. In May 1945, the American War Department drew up a memorandum for Jackson setting out the case that the major war criminals collectively 'entered into a common plan or enterprise aimed at the establishment of complete domination of Europe and eventually the world'.[18] In June, Jackson reported to President Truman his belief that the German leadership had indeed operated with a 'master plan', in which everything from the indoctrination of German youth to the muzzling of the trade unions had served the central grotesque ambition to wage criminal war on the world.[19] The conspiracy charge neatly removed the need to define new categories of crime for the other policies pursued by the regime, since they could, Jackson believed, all be subsumed under the heading of the master plan.

The conspiracy thesis provoked both scepticism and unease among the other prosecution teams. The first problem was simply one of evidence. The central document in the American case was Hitler's *Mein Kampf*, which was naively considered to be an outline of the future foreign policy of Hitler's Germany. A British Foreign Office analysis of the content of the book, writ-

---

[18] NA II, RG 107, McCloy papers, Box 3, draft Planning Memorandum, 13 May 1945, p. 2.

[19] NA II, RG 107, Stimson papers, Box 5, Bernays to Stimson, report to the President, 7 June 1945.

ten in June 1945, was forced to conclude that the book 'does not reveal the Nazi aims of conquest and domination fully and explicitly'.[20] The British argued that the Nazis were 'supreme opportunists', and thought it highly unlikely that the prosecution could make a conspiracy theory work, not only in law, but in terms of the available evidence. The second problem was the absence of any legal foundation for the charge of conspiring to wage aggressive war. Jackson insisted that such a foundation existed in the Kellogg–Briand Pact signed in Paris in 1928 by sixty-five signatory powers. The Pact was a statement of intent rather than a binding international convention, but the intent was clear enough: to renounce war as a means of settling disputes, except in the case of self-defence. It was signed by Germany, Japan, Italy and the Soviet Union, all of whom undertook wars of aggression at some point in the decade that followed. Its American sponsors declared that signature of the Pact heralded 'the outlawry of war'; this interpretation sustained Jackson's later argument that, under its terms, 'aggressive war-making is illegal and criminal'.[21]

---

[20] PRO, LCO 2/2900, Foreign Office memorandum, 'Nazism as a Conspiracy for the Domination of Europe', 22 June 1945, pp. 1–2.

[21] NA II, RG 107, report to the President, 7 June 1945, pp. 6–7. See also J. P. Kenny, *Moral Aspects of Nuremberg* (Washington DC, 1949), p. 6.

There were problems too with the French and Soviet approach to the trials. In neither state did the legal tradition support the idea of conspiracy. Whereas in Anglo-Saxon law it was possible to declare all those complicit with a conspiracy as equally responsible in law, in French and Soviet (and German) law the defendant had to be charged with a specific crime in which he had directly participated. The French preferred a trial based on particular atrocities and acts of terrorism, but this would have prevented the prosecution of most of those who ended up in the dock at Nuremberg. The Soviet legal experts, who had first invented the term 'crimes against peace', used later in the Indictment, were very concerned that 'conspiracy to wage aggressive war' should be confined only to the Axis states, and only to specific instances of violation: Poland in 1939, the Soviet Union in 1941, and so on. This anxiety masked more than legal niceties. If Jackson succeeded in making the waging of aggressive war into a substantive crime in international law, then the Soviet Union was equally guilty in its attacks on Poland in September 1939 and on Finland three months later. Jackson knew this. In his personal file on 'Aggression' were the terms of the German–Soviet agreement of 1939, dividing Poland. It was kept in the file and never presented at Nuremberg. The Soviet authorities ordered any discussion of aggression against Poland removed from the opening address of the Soviet prosecutor, and the Soviet courtroom team was under specific instructions to shout down any attempt by the defendants to raise awkward issues of Soviet–German collaboration.[22]

The result of these many objections was a compromise. Jackson agreed that the charge of conspiracy should only apply to specific acts of Axis aggression, and that other charges should be brought separately, not simply placed under the umbrella of a general conspiracy. But this still left the difficulty of how to include the terror and racism of the regime in any indictment. None of the prosecution teams wanted to focus only on the waging of war, and the crimes that resulted directly from it. In particular, the American and British prosecutors wanted to include Nazi anti-semitism as an indictable offence. The difficulty in doing so was highlighted when an academic judgment was sought on how to define Nazi racial and national persecution in law. Rafael Lemkin coined a new term 'genocide' to describe the intention to 'cripple in their

22 NA II, RG 238, Box 32, aggression file. See also S. Mironenko, 'La collection des documents sur le procès de Nuremberg dans les archives d'état de la fédération russe', in A. Wiewiorka (ed.), *Les procès de Nuremberg et de Tokyo* (Paris, 1996), pp. 65–6.

development, or destroy completely, entire nations', but he concluded that this could not apply to the Jews, who were not a nation, and he omitted anti-semitism in his suggested list of cases in which 'genocide' had occurred.[23] Since both the French and Soviet prosecutors were anxious to include the persecution of their populations in the trial proceedings, a new category of offence, 'crimes against humanity', was agreed. Under the terms of these crimes could be included the deliberate persecution and murder of Jews, gypsies and Poles.

The most powerful legal objection was never properly confronted. The crimes of which the defendants stood accused were not regarded as crimes when they were committed, with the exception of war crimes as defined under international agreement. Robert Ley began his rejection of the legal basis of the tribunal by pointing out that the declaration establishing the Tribunal, issued on 8 August 1945, created laws '*after all* the crimes mentioned in the indictment, which they wish to judge, had been committed'.[24] The idea of retrospective justice was foreign to most legal traditions. The idea that the Tribunal would be both legislator and judge, creating crimes in order to punish them, was

---

[23] NA II, RG 238, Judge Advocate's papers, memorandum for General John Weir from Rafael Lemkin, 14 July 1945, pp. 3–14.
[24] NA II, RG 238, Jackson main files, Box 3, Ley to Pflücker, p. 1.

something that Western legal opinion also found difficult to accept. When the Acting Dean of the Harvard
Law School was asked for an opinion on the conspiracy
charge, he argued that retrospective justice was alien to
the spirit of 'Anglo-American legal thought', and urged
its rejection as 'unwise and unjustifiable'.[25] The
Professor of International Law at London University, H.
A. Smith, writing in December 1945, argued that the
Tribunal was to be treated as a 'special case', which self-
consciously departed from the principle 'that a man
must not be punished for an act which did not constitute a crime at the time when it was committed'. Only
time would show whether this 'very serious' decision
was 'right or wrong'.[26]

Jackson was quite aware of these objections. When he
prepared his first report on the plans for a trial for
Truman in June 1945, he argued that, even if they were
not designated crimes, the acts committed by the Axis
enemy 'have been regarded as criminal since the time of
Cain'.[27] The argument in favour of retrospective justice
rested on the idea that many of the acts covered by the

[25] NA II, RG 107, McCloy papers, Box 3, 'Morgan's Opinion on
      Conspiracy Theory', 12 January 1945, pp. 2–4.
[26] H. A. Smith, 'The Great Experiment at Nuremberg', *The Listener*,
      vol. 34, 13 December 1945, p. 694.
[27] NA II, RG 107, Stimson papers, Box 5, Bernays to Stimson, 7
      June 1945, pp. 4–5.

Indictment were in fact known to be criminal at the time they were committed, and would have been subject to criminal proceedings had the law not been perverted by dictatorship. These were flimsy arguments, but the central purpose of the Tribunal was not to conform to existing principles in international law but to establish new rules of international conduct and agreed boundaries in the violation of human rights. The Indictment formally issued on 19 October 1945 consisted of four charges: a common conspiracy to wage aggressive war; crimes against peace; war crimes; and crimes against humanity. At least one of the four prosecuting states, the Soviet Union, was guilty on three of the four counts for acts it had wilfully committed on its own behalf during the previous decade.

The conduct of the trial betrayed the improvised and ambiguous character of its origin. There were practical issues that had not been anticipated. The time taken to translate documents in evidence and other trial material into French and Russian meant that the prosecution teams often lacked the papers they needed, or received them at the last moment. Defence lawyers had particular difficulty in obtaining access to material necessary for the presentation of their defence. All the prosecution teams were short of skilled translators and interpreters, which compounded the problem. The sheer volume of accumulated evidence made it certain that the trial would take considerably longer than had at first been intended. In the summer of 1945, it was hoped that a trial could be started in September and might be over by Christmas. A speedy trial was felt to be desirable to satisfy Allied public opinion that justice was being done as swiftly as judicial process would allow.[28] In reality, the trial lasted for almost a year, and it proved difficult to sustain popular interest in its outcome.

It was also difficult to mask the extent to which the trial was governed by political as much as by legal considerations. The Soviet authorities made no pretence that they considered all the defendants guilty *a priori*. The trial was regarded as a show-trial, in which Nazi leaders would be exposed to public disapproval before execution. Stalin established a government commission 'on the direction of the Nuremberg trial', which oversaw efforts to ensure that nothing hostile to Soviet interests would be exposed by the court. In November 1945, the NKVD sent Colonel Likhachev to Nuremberg to win the support of the other three prosecution teams in avoiding awkward questions about Soviet foreign policy.[29] The other powers tolerated

[28] PRO, FO 1019/82, Maxwell Fyfe to Jackson, 21 September 1945, p. 2.
[29] A. Vaksberg, *The Prosecutor and the Prey: Vyshinsky and the 1930s Moscow Show Trials* (London, 1990), pp. 258–9.

the pressure, though in the notorious case of the Katyn massacre of Polish soldiers the British authorities were, rightly, convinced that this had been a Soviet, not a Nazi atrocity. At one point during the trial, the Soviet Procurator-General, Andrei Vyshinsky, guest-of-honour at a dinner for the Tribunal judges, compelled his companions to raise their glasses in a macabre toast to the defendants: 'May their paths lead straight from the court-house to the grave!'[30] This was a difficult position for American and British judges, who could scarcely endorse the imminent execution of men they were supposed to be treating with judicial impartiality.

Nonetheless, the three Western powers all came to accept the Soviet position that Allied actions which might now be regarded as crimes as a result of the new categories defined by the Tribunal should be excluded from review. Throughout the trial there was only one brief mention of the Soviet–Finnish war, and this was shouted down. Bombing was not included as a war crime, despite the fact that large numbers of innocent civilians were killed on both sides. Even while the horrors of the Nazi camp system were being revealed in court, the Soviet authorities were setting up concentration camps in the Soviet zone of occupation, like the

[30]   T. Taylor, *The Anatomy of the Nuremberg Trials: A Personal Memoir* (London, 1993), p. 211.

isolation camp at Mühlberg on the Elbe, where, out of 122,000 prisoners who were sent without trial to the camp, over 43,000 were killed or died.[31]

This collaboration was sustained in the face of the emerging Cold War for several reasons. It was important for the Western states that the trial did not break down into inter-Allied bickering, and that the Soviet Union was not exposed as an international criminal. The hypocrisy was sustained on grounds of *Realpolitik*. The whole purpose of the trial, as a statement about international morality and human rights, would have been destroyed, and Nazi crimes viewed with an unwanted moral relativism, if the situation had been otherwise. The political purpose of the trials was also evident in the efforts to use them as part of a more general programme of re-education in Germany, and, by implication, in the rest of Europe. In one of the pre-trial interrogations, the American interrogator, Howard Brundage, explained to his interviewee, the diplomat Fritz Wiedemann, what he believed the trials represented:

> We are trying to get up a record here for the benefit of the children of Germany, so that, when another time comes and a gang like this gets control of the

31 A. Kilian, *Einzuweisen zur völligen Isolierung. NKWD-Speziallager Mühlberg/Elbe 1945–1948* (Leipzig, 1993), p. 7.

> government, they will have something to look back
> on and be warned in advance ... [T]he United States
> doesn't expect anything out of this, and we are
> anxious to make a record here that will be a lesson to
> the German people.[32]

The assumption of Western moral superiority implicit in the liberal values expressed in the Indictment was accepted as a necessary underpinning for the construction of a new moral and political order.

There were also legal problems raised by the trial. The provision of evidence was far from ideal. Vital material on the genocide of the Jews only emerged with the capture of the commandant of Auschwitz, Rudolf Höss, in March 1946, and his testimony arrived too late to be included fully in the trial proceedings. The Soviet Union provided unsworn written depositions about German atrocities in the east, but refused to allow Soviet citizens to be called as witnesses at Nuremberg. In the early summer of 1945, Jackson's team circulated a secret memorandum making it clear that it was inexpedient to wait until all the material for trial had been gathered together, and that the case should rest on 'the *best* evidence readily available'.[33] The whole idea of

[32] Imperial War Museum, FO 645, Box 162, interrogation of Fritz Wiedemann, taken at Nuremberg, 9 October 1945, pp. 22–3.

[33] NA II, RG 107, McCloy papers, Box 3, draft Planning Memorandum, 13 May 1945, pp. 3–5.

conspiracy did prove difficult to demonstrate, and in the end three of the defendants, von Papen, Schacht and Fritzsche, were found not-guilty on all four counts. Subsequent historical research has confirmed that no such thing as a concerted conspiracy existed, though a mass of additional evidence on the atrocities of the regime and the widespread complicity of many officials, judges and soldiers in these crimes has confirmed that, despite all the drawbacks of the trial and of its legal foundation, the conviction that this was a criminal system was in no sense misplaced.

The Nuremberg trials were an experiment. There was a clear international consensus among the victor powers that the perpetrators of aggression should this time be treated differently by the international community. To be able to conduct such an experiment it was necessary to have an agreed set of rules of conduct in international affairs and on fundamental issues of human rights. The precise nature of the crimes associated with the war had to be defined and given clear legal status. What is striking about the summer of 1945 is not that the trials were in some sense arbitrary and in defiance of legal convention, but that so much was achieved in the chaos of post-war Europe in building the foundation for contemporary international law on war crimes, and contemporary conventions on human rights. The International

Criminal Court established in 2002 is a direct descendant of the Nuremberg Military Tribunal, as were the European Convention on Human Rights signed in 1950 and the genocide convention two years earlier. The trials were without question a political act, agreed at the level of diplomacy, and motivated by political interests. The choice of defendants and the definition of the charges were arbitrary in the extreme, and rested on endless wrangles between the prosecution teams and governments of the four Allied states. Yet the final outcome was less prejudiced and more self-evidently just than these objections might imply. The trial did not fabricate the reality of the Third Reich and the death of as many as seven million men, women and children murdered or allowed to die by the apparatus of state repression, or the deaths of many millions more, Germans among them, from the waging of continental war. After this grotesque historical experience, few could doubt, either then or now, that the international community required new legal instruments to cope with its possible recurrence. The fact that in many cases since 1945 it has proved impossible to prevent or anticipate further violations is not a consequence of the failure of the Nuremberg experiment, nor of the legal apparatus that it spawned. It is a consequence of a persistent reality in which power will always tend to triumph over justice.

2

Issues of complexity, complicity and complementarity: from the Nuremberg trials to the dawn of the new International Criminal Court

ANDREW CLAPHAM

Introduction

The International Criminal Court came into existence on 1 July 2002. The new Court has jurisdiction over genocide, crimes against humanity and war crimes; but the Court can only try international crimes committed on or after 1 July 2002. Any national, from any of the more than eighty states that have ratified the Statute of the Court, can be a potential defendant before the new Court. In addition, the Court will have jurisdiction over crimes committed in state parties, even when perpetrated by nationals from states which have not become parties to the Statute. There are further grounds for jurisdiction but we need not dwell on them here. In this contribution I shall remain with the theme of the Nuremberg trials and use these trials as a springboard to explore three concepts which I think may help us to think about the ways in which the new International Criminal Court will operate. The three concepts I wish to explore are: complexity, complicity and complementarity.

Complexity

To understand what I mean by complexity in this context, let us consider some of the fundamental legal innovations of the Nuremberg judgment delivered by the International Military Tribunal. First, the notion of individuals having concrete duties under international law, as opposed to national law, was clearly enunciated, really for the first time, and later accepted by the international community of states. Until the Nuremberg trial, war crimes trials had been held at the national level under national military law. The international laws of war, such as the Hague Convention of 1907, already prohibited resort to certain methods of waging war. But, in the words of the judgment:

> the Hague Convention nowhere designates such
> practices as criminal, nor is any sentence
> prescribed, nor any mention made of a court to try
> and punish offenders.[1]

[1] *Trial of German Major War Criminals (Goering et al.)*, International Military Tribunal (Nuremberg), Judgment and

The judges, in a remarkable bout of judicial activism, decided that:

> The law of war is to be found not only in treaties, but in the customs and practices of states which gradually obtained universal recognition, and from general principles of justice applied by jurists, and practised by military courts. This law is not static, but by continual adaptation follows the needs of a changing world. Indeed, in many cases treaties do no more than express and define for more accurate reference the principles of law already existing.[2]

In this way the Tribunal held that, even though the international treaties they were applying made no mention of criminal law, the international law of war created international crimes.

The defence had further argued that international law did not apply to individuals but only to states. The Tribunal, in a famous passage, rejected this argument as well. In the words of the Tribunal:

> Many other authorities could be cited, but enough has been said to show that individuals can be punished for violations of international law. Crimes against international law are committed by

Sentence, 30 September and 1 October 1946 (Cmd 6964, HMSO, London), p. 40; the judgment is also reproduced in (1947) 41 *American Journal of International Law* 172–333.

[2] *Goering et al.*, note 1 above, p. 40.

> men, not by abstract entities, and only by punishing individuals who commit such crimes can the provisions of international law be enforced.[3]

It was, in retrospect, a very radical moment in the history of human rights and humanitarian law. There was a paradigm shift. It was the beginning of a new way of thinking about international law as going beyond obligations on states and attaching duties to individuals involving criminal responsibility. Human rights law would later come to create duties for individuals beyond the types of crimes tried at Nuremberg. More specifically, human rights law developed around the prohibitions on genocide, torture, disappearances and summary executions, so that it is possible to consider individual responsibility for these human rights violations, even in the absence of an armed conflict.

These developments may seem now eminently sensible, even unremarkable, but the situation is *complex* for a lawyer, because the same act and the same provision of international law give rise to multiple responsibilities. We have, first, the responsibility of the state under international law for the violation of its international obligations under a treaty or customary obligation on the laws of war, and then, secondly, we simultaneously have the

---

3   *Ibid.*, p. 41.

responsibility of the individual for violating the same law. But the complexity does not end there.

In Nuremberg there was a determination, not only to try individuals, but, at the same trial, to declare certain organisations to be criminal organisations. In this way individuals could later be prosecuted and punished for past membership of such organisations. Thus the Tribunal declared criminal the leadership corps of the Nazi Party, the Gestapo, the SD and the SS.[4]

In fact, in drawing up the list of defendants at Nuremberg, as was explained by Professor Overy in the first lecture in this series, the Prosecutor selected the individuals according to their connections to the organisations which were also targeted in the trial. The organisations even had their own counsel appointed by the Tribunal to represent them at the trial. As was also mentioned by Professor Overy, it was not only the political organisations which concerned the prosecutors and judges: there was also a determination to ensure that German industry, and the industrialists who had supported the German war effort, were also exposed and punished. This adds to the complexity of the proceedings. Not only did international law reach states, government ministers, individual military

4   The SD is the *Sicherheitsdeinst des Reichführer SS*, and the SS is the *Schutzstaffen*.

officers, certain political parties and public entities, but there was also an intention to reach into the private sector and punish private industrialists and, in a way, the firms themselves.

One of the original indictees at Nuremberg was the industrialist from the Krupp company, Gustav Krupp von Bohlen und Halbach. He was an old man when the trial started and he was said by his lawyers to be unfit for trial due to senile dementia. The Tribunal ordered medical examinations, and, even though he could not respond to simple commands such as 'turn your head from left to right', the Tribunal refused to drop him from the indictment. The British Prosecutor strongly objected to any change or delay, citing 'the interests of justice'. On the other hand, the US Prosecutor had been prepared to substitute Krupp von Bohlen's son, Alfried, on the Indictment. This is an odd idea at first sight, but the documents reveal the extent to which justice was to be served by prosecuting the Krupp firm, rather than the individual, even in a situation where the Tribunal only had jurisdiction over individuals. The US answer drafted by Robert Jackson stated:

> Public interests, which transcend all private
> considerations, require that Krupp von Bohlen
> shall not be dismissed unless some other
> representative of the Krupp armament and

munitions industry be substituted. These public
interests are as follows:

Four generations of the Krupp family have
owned and operated the great armament and
munitions plants which have been the chief source
of Germany's war supplies. For over 130 years this
family has been the focus, the symbol, and the
beneficiary of the most sinister forces engaged in
menacing the peace of Europe. During the period
between the two World Wars, the management of
these enterprises was chiefly in Defendant Krupp
von Bohlen.

It was at all times, however, a Krupp family
enterprise. Only a nominal owner himself, Von
Bohlen's wife, Bertha Krupp, owned the bulk of the
stock. About 1937 their son, Alfried Krupp, became
plant manager and was actively associated in the
policy-making and executive management
thereafter …

To drop Krupp von Bohlen from this case
without substitution of Alfried, drops from the case
the entire Krupp family, and defeats any effective
judgment against the German armament makers.[5]

The British Prosecutor strongly objected to any
substitution or delay. In the words of the Chief
Prosecutor:

[5] Answer of the United States Prosecution to the Motion on
Behalf of Defendant Gustav Krupp von Bohlen, Robert Jackson,
12 November 1945, available at www.yale.edu/lawweb/avalon/
imt/proc/v1-11.htm.

> Although in an ordinary case it is undesirable that a defendant should be tried when he is unable to comprehend the charges made against him, or to give instructions for his defence, there are special considerations which apply to this case.[6]

According to the British Chief Prosecutor, one of the interests of justice, referred to in the Charter of the Tribunal in the context of trials in the absence of the accused,[7] was the public interest in trying the defendant responsible for the preparation of armaments and using forced labour from the concentration camps.

The Tribunal's eventual decision was that Gustav Krupp could not be tried because of his condition, but that 'the charges against him in the Indictment should be retained for trial thereafter, if the physical and mental condition of the defendant should permit'.[8] However, his son Alfried was later tried with eleven others from the Krupp firm by the US Military Tribunal

---

[6] Memorandum of the British Prosecution on the Motion on Behalf of Defendant Gustav Krupp von Bohlen, 12 November 1945, Sir Hartley Shawcross, available at www.yale.edu/lawweb/avalon/imt/proc/v1-12.htm.

[7] Article 12: 'The Tribunal shall have the right to take proceedings against a person charged with crimes set out in Article 6 of this Charter in his absence, if he has not been found or if the Tribunal, for any reason, finds it necessary, in the interests of justice, to conduct the hearing in his absence.'

[8] *Goering et al.*, note 1 above, p. 2.

in Nuremberg and Alfried received a twelve-year sentence for plunder and employing prisoners of war and foreign civilians under inhumane conditions in connection with the conduct of war.

In Alfried Krupp's case, the defence lawyers suggested that international law did not attach to private industrialists who did not act on behalf of the state. They sought to distinguish the Tribunal's judgment in *Goering et al.*, concerning the responsibility of the individual, by claiming that these individuals had been state agents:

> One must consider, however, that, in the case of the International Military Tribunal, the persons involved were not private individuals such as those appearing in this case, but responsible officials of the State, that is such persons and only such persons as, by virtue of their office, acted on behalf of the State. It may be a much healthier point of view not to adhere in all circumstances to the text of the provisions of International law, which is, in itself, abundantly clear, but rather to follow the spirit of that law, and to state that anyone who acted on behalf of the state is liable to punishment under the terms of penal law, because, as an anonymous subject, the State itself cannot be held responsible for the compensation of damage. In no circumstances is it permissible, however, to hold criminally responsible a private individual, an industrialist in this case, who has not acted on behalf of the State, who was not an official or an

> organ of the State, and of whom, furthermore, in
> the face of the theory of law as it has been
> understood up to this time, and as it is outlined
> above, it is impossible to ascertain that he had any
> idea, and who, in fact, had no idea that he, together
> with his State, was under an obligation to ensure
> adherence to the provisions of international law.[9]

The prosecution dealt with this:

> It has also been suggested that International Law is
> a vague and complicated thing and that private
> industrialists should be given the benefit of the plea
> of ignorance of the law. Whatever weight, if any,
> such a defence might have in other circumstances
> and with other defendants, we think it would be
> quite preposterous to give it any weight in this case.
> We are not dealing here with small businessmen,
> unsophisticated in the ways of the world or lacking
> in capable legal counsel. Krupp was one of the great
> international industrial institutions with numerous
> connections in many countries, and constantly
> engaged in international commercial intercourse.[10]

As stated above, the result for Alfried Krupp was an
eventual sentence of twelve years' imprisonment.

Although the defence that international law is a

[9]   Case No. 58, *Trial of Alfried Felix Alwyn Krupp von Bohlen und
      Halbach and eleven others*, US Military Tribunal, Nuremberg, 17
      November 1947 to 30 June 1948, *Law Reports of Trials of War
      Criminals*, vol. X, p. 69 at p. 170.
[10] *Ibid.*

'vague and complicated thing' did not succeed, it is worth recalling the layers of complexity we have discussed. First, we have to admit that the crimes prosecuted in Nuremberg were not actually formulated as crimes with the specificity we would expect in a criminal trial. The Tribunal was, as we saw, inspired by treaties, the 'customs and practices of states' and the 'general principles of justice applied by jurists and practised by military courts'.[11] Secondly, this complicated thing called international law worked, not only to create obligations for states, but also to create duties for individuals from public and private life, as well as obligations for their organisations.

How has this complexity been addressed in the fifty years since Nuremberg? The Tokyo trial in 1946 dealt with essentially similar crimes, although the Charter for that Tribunal was more terse in its listing of crimes. Article 5 listed the acts which came within the jurisdiction of the Tokyo Tribunal. Article 5(b) is headed

[11] The London Charter included the following definition: 'Article 6(b) WAR CRIMES: namely, violations of the laws or customs of war. Such violations shall include, but not be limited to, murder, ill-treatment or deportation to slave labor or for any other purpose of civilian population of or in occupied territory, murder or ill-treatment of prisoners of war or persons on the seas, killing of hostages, plunder of public or private property, wanton destruction of cities, towns or villages, or devastation not justified by military necessity.'

'Conventional War Crimes', which is then defined as 'violations of the laws and customs of war'. The simplicity of this definition masks the complexity of the detail of what actually constitutes a violation of the laws and customs of war. So, the Charter of the Tokyo Tribunal offered little assistance in dealing with the first layer of complexity by failing to specify the actual crimes it was concerned with. With regard to the second dimension, there was no development at all. The Tokyo Tribunal did not deal with issues of criminal organisations or with the question of the Japanese industrialists, the *zaibatsu*.[12]

Following the Nuremberg and Tokyo precedents, we have to wait almost fifty years for further international criminal trials. In the 1990s, two new international criminal tribunals were created by the UN Security Council: first, in 1993, the International Criminal Tribunal for the former Yugoslavia, and, secondly, in 1994, the International Criminal Tribunal for Rwanda. These Tribunals developed the scope of international criminal law even further. By this time we have the extra

[12] For differing views on why the Japanese industrialists were not included, see A. C. Brackman, *The Other Nuremberg: The Untold Story of the Tokyo War Crimes Trials* (Collins, London, 1989), p. 208; and B. V. A. Röling and A. Cassese, *The Tokyo Trial and Beyond: Reflections of a Peacemonger* (Polity Press, Cambridge, 1993), p. 39.

specificity of the Genocide Convention of 1948 and of the 1949 Geneva Conventions and their Protocols of 1977. They in turn developed the scope of genocide as a crime against humanity and extended international responsibility into situations of internal armed conflict. The category of crimes against humanity had first been introduced into the Nuremberg Charter to ensure that the deportation of Germans by Germans to the concentration camps and their subsequent mistreatment and extermination there could be prosecuted. Under the international laws of war at that time, the way a government treated its own nationals was considered by international law as a matter of domestic jurisdiction rather than international concern. The introduction of this new sort of international crime was important. However, it was introduced in a rather limited way: for the Nuremberg and Tokyo Tribunals to have jurisdiction over an accused, charges of crimes against humanity had to be linked to the armed conflict.[13] It has been

13 The Articles concerning crimes against humanity in both Tribunals specified that the crimes had to be committed 'in execution of or in connection with any crime within the jurisdiction of the Tribunal'. The Nuremberg Charter contained an additional requirement that the acts be committed against 'any civilian population', the Tokyo Charter having been amended to delete this requirement. Although the Statute of the International Criminal Court does not require that the crime against humanity be linked to an armed conflict, the Statute

said by one of the judges from the Tokyo Tribunal that the requirement that crimes against humanity be linked to the armed conflict was introduced because some Americans were, and I quote Judge Röling from the Tokyo Tribunal, 'afraid that, without this new element, the new crime would be applicable to the mistreatment of Blacks in the US!'[14]

Fifty years later, the Yugoslavia and Rwanda Tribunals have clearly established that crimes against humanity exist as self-standing crimes. These international crimes can be prosecuted even in the absence of an armed conflict. This new understanding of crimes against humanity has, in a way, elevated systematic human rights violations to the level of international crimes. In fact, the International Law Commission's 1991 text on Crimes Against the Peace and Security of Mankind used the expression 'systematic or mass violations of human rights' in the Article which eventually became Article 18 ('Crimes against humanity') of the Draft Code finally adopted by the ILC in 1996.

retains the requirement that it be directed against a civilian population. It is possible that crimes against humanity targeted at military personnel are crimes under international law, although it is more likely these would be prosecuted as war crimes in the context of an armed conflict.

[14] B. V. A. Röling and A. Cassese, *The Tokyo Trial and Beyond: Reflections of a Peacemonger* (Polity Press, Cambridge, 1993), p. 55.

In the context of the Rwanda trials, the reach of international criminal law has been confirmed to apply to individuals who were not necessarily part of the armed forces. It is enough to have been the mayor of a village and to have encouraged rapes simply by one's presence; it is enough to be the director of a tea plantation and to allow trucks to be used to hunt down and exterminate civilians. In the last situation, a Trial Chamber of the International Criminal Tribunal for Rwanda in January 2000 found Mr Musema criminally responsible for such acts. Having been arrested in 1995 in Switzerland and transferred to the International Criminal Tribunal for Rwanda in Tanzania, the Chamber found him guilty of genocide and crimes against humanity. For these crimes there was no need for a connection to an armed conflict. He was given a life sentence. Aggravating circumstances which were raised at the sentencing stage included the fact that he took no steps to prevent the participation of the tea factory employees or the use of its vehicles in the attacks.

> 898. With respect to the Prosecutor's argument that Musema could also be held responsible under Article 6(3) of the Statute, the Chamber finds, first, that among the attackers at Rwirambo were persons identified as employees of the Gisovu Tea Factory. The Chamber is of the view that their participation resulted, inevitably, in the commission of acts referred to under Articles 2 to 4 of the Statute,

including, in particular, causing serious bodily and mental harm to members of the Tutsi group.

899. The Chamber finds that it has also been established, as held *supra*, that Musema was the superior of said employees and that he held not only *de jure* power over them, but also *de facto* power. Noting that Musema was personally present at the attack sites, the Chamber is of the opinion that he knew or, at least, had reason to know that his subordinates were about to commit such acts or had done so. The Chamber notes that Musema, nevertheless, failed to take the necessary and reasonable measures to prevent the commission of said acts by his subordinates, but rather abetted in their commission, by his presence and by his personal participation.

900. Consequently, the Chamber finds that, for the acts committed by the employees of the Gisovu Tea Factory during the attack on Rwirambo Hill, Musema incurs individual criminal responsibility, as their superior, on the basis of Article 6(3) of the Statute.[15]

So the complexity of this type of international criminal law extends past individual states, political parties and state agents on towards individual private industrialists and business people with *de facto* control over their subordinates, and finally even towards their firms.

As we saw above, there was a concern in the work of

[15] *Alfred Musema Case*, ICTR-96-13-T, 27 January 2000.

the Nuremberg Tribunal to ensure the Krupp firm was addressed as such. In 1946 the Farben company was actually considered an instrumentality of its directors in their commission of war crimes and was implicated in the conviction of the directors by the US Military Tribunal in Nuremberg. The same Farben company has much more recently been subject to claims for reparations from the victims of their practices of slave labour. The German slave labour fund, jointly established by the state and the firms, currently stands at US$5.2 billion. These claims, together with similar claims made against the Swiss banks in the Holocaust victims' assets litigation (which has resulted in a fund of US$1.25 billion), are based on the law developed during the Nuremberg trials of the industrialists and its application in the US courts. By 1999, more than thirty cases were brought against US, German and Swiss companies alleging complicity in Nazi-era crimes, based on the original trials of the industrialists in Nuremberg. The latest round of claims concerns Swiss and US banks with regard to profits from business in South Africa from 1948 to 1993. The reported demand is for US$50 billion.[16]

How does the new International Criminal Court

[16] 'Banks Sued for Financing S. Africa's Apartheid Regime', *Financial Times*, 18 June 2002, p. 8.

(ICC) respond to these complexities? First, the new Court has clarified much of the confusion surrounding the rather vague nature of the crimes tried in Nuremberg and Tokyo, and it has included the new wider jurisdiction for crimes against humanity eliminating any need for a connection to the armed conflict. For the new Court, crimes against humanity are acts committed in a widespread or systematic way with an organisational policy against any civilian population, where the acts are, among other things, murder, enslavement, deportation or forcible transfer of population, imprisonment in violation of international law, torture, persecution, enforced disappearance and the crime of apartheid. All the ICC crimes (with the exception of aggression, which is still to be defined) are now listed as individual crimes with the elements of these crimes listed in a separate document. Rather than the terse sentence asserting jurisdiction over violations of the 'laws and customs of war', we now have several pages of war crimes listed in a way which renders them quite specific. Although some students and defendants may still complain that this international law is a vague and complicated thing, it is now at least written down in a treaty and accessible to everyone.

With regard to the second dimension of complexity, that is to say the range of actors addressed by the law, the new Court will address only part of the picture. Only individuals can be tried in the new Court. It will not be possible to bring cases against states, nor will there be cases against political organisations or companies. There was considerable discussion during the Rome Conference as to whether the Court should have jurisdiction over organisations as well as individuals. In the end there was no time to formulate a provision which would have been acceptable to the large majority of states.[17] Nevertheless, as more and more states adopt legislation to enable co-operation with the new Court, it is quite possible that this legislation is adapted to allow for prosecutions of corporations or other organisations. I might repeat that the contemporary claims brought against Germany and the German companies over the last decade can be traced back to the Nuremberg trials, and in one case to the actual findings against industrialists from the Farben company. One might imagine that, in the future, successful prosecutions against individuals in the new International

[17] I have explained the details of this part of the negotiations in A. Clapham, 'The Question of Jurisdiction under International Criminal Law over Legal Persons: Lessons from the Rome Conference on an International Criminal Court', in M. Kamminga and S. Zia-Zarifi (eds.), *Liability of Multinational Corporations under International Law* (Kluwer Law International, The Hague, 2000), pp. 139–95.

Criminal Court could generate similar settlements against states, their organisations or even their firms.

The new Court does have the power to make orders concerning reparations and restitution. But no one expects many defendants to arrive in The Hague with healthy, traceable bank accounts or property in their name. Nevertheless, the Rome Statute is careful to state in Article 75(6) that nothing with regard to the Court's own orders for reparations against individuals shall be interpreted as prejudicing the rights of victims under national or international law. Such parallel claims by victims for compensation or restitution will take place in multiple fora, illustrating perhaps a third level of complexity.

This third layer of complexity reminds us that international criminal law is enforced not only in the international tribunals set up to try the most serious cases but also at the national level in national courts: these might be the national courts of the perpetrator, the national courts where the acts took place, the national courts of the victims or even the national courts where the perpetrator is arrested.

To summarise, I have highlighted three levels of complexity: first, the rather unspecified and evolving nature of the crimes; secondly, the multiple actors and entities who are addressed by this type of criminal law;

and, thirdly, the fact that trials and claims can take place in various fora at both the international and national levels.

Complicity

Let me turn to my second concept, complicity.[18] This concept is familiar in both national and international criminal law. Rather than compare multiple legal systems, I want to discuss why we need to rely on such a concept and how it is being used today by those concerned about violations of human rights and humanitarian law. The concept is being used to frame claims which go beyond a simple application of contemporary criminal law. The point is that, when different actors label a certain activity 'complicity', they deliberately evoke conceptions of criminality and blameworthiness even if, strictly speaking, the activity would not give rise to criminal liability in a court of law. Why are we witnessing such a strain on the complicity concept?

I want to suggest that, at the international level, there is a recognition that simple rules attributing conduct to

18 For a detailed discussion, see W. Schabas, 'Enforcing International Humanitarian Law: Catching the Accomplices' (2001) 83 *Review of the International Committee of the Red Cross* 439–59.

single actors fail to capture the *complexity* of the phenomena we are trying to tackle.

For any illegal act, there is often a sense that, even if one starts by thinking about the principal perpetrator, there is a need to consider others who finance, facilitate, encourage, support and assist in the enterprise. Following the events of 11 September 2001, it was obvious that the principal perpetrators were all dead. But one only has to turn up any political speech around that time to see the focus on 'complicity' and the search for the 'accomplices' of those who carried out the attacks. We have since seen the extension of the so-called 'war' on terrorism to those accused of aiding, abetting or harbouring terrorists. And, as we saw above in the context of the claims against the Swiss banks and the German industrialists, there is currently considerable legal activity focused on the extension of international criminal responsibility beyond those who perpetrate international crimes to those who facilitate such crimes by financing them.

Thinking about accomplices is nothing new at the national level. But transposing some of the principles to the international level is not obvious. First, while at the national level most actors have more or less the same obligations under the criminal law, at the international level different actors have different responsibilities under international law, and these obligations can vary from state to state, even with regard to the laws of war. Secondly, where someone assists a perpetrator to commit an act which is not criminal in the state where the act is perpetrated but which is criminal in the state where the act was prepared, we enter tricky transnational terrain.[19]

But I want to step back a bit and consider some fundamental questions about our sense of responsibility when faced with human rights violations committed in other countries. The sense that we cannot stand idly by lest we be complicit through our inaction is more and more a theme in international relations. Pierre Hazan, in his book, *La Justice face à la guerre: de Nuremberg à la Haye*, quotes a former French foreign minister, Roland Dumas, explaining his position when faced with mounting public opinion that something should be done in reaction to the bombardment of Sarajevo and the ongoing sniper attacks:

> Je ne voulais pas me trouver dans la situation de l'après-Seconde Guerre mondiale, où le monde découvre les camps de la mort, et rien n'est pensé pour punir les coupables. Je voulais qu'au moins,

---

19 C. Forcese, 'Deterring "Militarized Commerce": The Prospect of Liability for "Privatized" Human Rights Abuses' (1999) 31 *Ottawa Law Review* 171–221.

> d'une manière ou d'une autre, ils aient à repondre à
> la justice, puisque nous ne voulions déjà pas
> intervenir militairement en Bosnie. Je ne voulais
> pas que l'on apparaisse comme des complices de
> crimes qui étaient encore en train d'être commis.[20]

The power of the complicity concept tells us more in this context about solidarity among peoples and a contemporary sense of responsibility through omission than it does about criminal law. Clearly, there were no real prospects of a criminal trial of a foreign minister of a Permanent Member of the Security Council as an accomplice to genocide in the former Yugoslavia. But the sense that we could be accused of complicity through our inaction or silence is a powerful modern-day concept. Complicity has another dimension, as is illustrated by the desire to reach down and catch the perpetrators at the level of the camp commanders. Thinking about complicity therefore reminds us all of our own role as well as broadening the scope of our inquiry into the network of those who facilitate, plan and perpetrate the violations of human rights and humanitarian law.

The concept of complicity is at the heart of contemporary questions of morality and ethics. As political and economic life becomes more diffuse with decisions

[20] P. Hazan, *La justice face à la guerre* (Stock, Paris, 2000), p. 38.

being taken at various levels of proximity from us, we may wonder how complicit we are in wrongdoing through our action or inaction. In a book entitled *Complicity*, Christopher Kutz introduces his subject in the following way:[21]

> Try as we might to live well, we find ourselves connected to harms and wrongs, albeit by relations that fall outside the paradigm of individual, intentional wrongdoing. Here are some examples: buying a table made of tropical wood that comes from a defoliated rainforest, or owning stock in a company that does business in a country that jails political dissenters; being a citizen of a nation that bombs another country's factories in a reckless attack on terrorists, or inhabiting a region seized long ago from its aboriginal occupants; helping to design an automobile the manufacturer knowingly sells with a dangerously defective fuel system, or administering a national health care bureaucracy that carelessly allows the distribution of HIV-contaminated blood.

For Kutz these examples fall in a moral grey zone: 'Although in each of these cases we stand outside the shadow of evil, we still do not find the full light of the good.'[22] His modern look at the legal and moral

[21] C. Kutz, *Complicity: Ethics and Law for a Collective Age* (Cambridge University Press, Cambridge, 2000), p. 1.
[22] *Ibid.*

dimensions of complicity forces us to consider our expanding notions of community, as our actions often have effects far beyond our immediate surroundings, and affect people to whom we may now have an increasing sense of responsibility. Of course, complicity in war crimes in the context of the Nuremberg trials has a specific legal meaning. In strict legal terms, for an international criminal trial, the accomplice liability test in international criminal law was summarised by the Trial Chamber of the International Criminal Tribunal for the former Yugoslavia (ICTY) in the *Tadic* case:

> The most relevant sources for such a determination are the Nürnberg war crimes trials, which resulted in several convictions for complicitous conduct. While the judgments generally failed to discuss in detail the criteria upon which guilt was determined, a clear pattern does emerge upon an examination of the relevant cases. First, there is a requirement of intent, which involves awareness of the act of participation coupled with a conscious decision to participate by planning, instigating, ordering, committing, or otherwise aiding and abetting in the commission of a crime. Secondly, the prosecution must prove that there was participation in that the conduct of the accused contributed to the commission of the illegal act.[23]

---

[23] *Prosecutor* v. *Dusko Tadic*, Case No. IT-94-1-T, Opinion and Judgment of the Trial Chamber, 7 May 1997, para. 674.

The new International Criminal Court's Statute includes accomplice liability not only for those who aid and abet, but also for those who 'otherwise assist'. The complicity concept in the Statute is designed to cover those who act 'for the purpose of facilitating' crimes. There is, however, no requirement in the Statute for the accomplice to make a direct or substantial contribution to the commission of crime.[24]

In sum, at least for international crimes already within the ICC Statute (genocide, crimes against humanity, and war crimes), the Statute defines the boundaries of complicity in a wide way, casting the net well beyond the principal perpetrators.

After a detailed review of the international law on individual accomplice liability, Professor Bill Schabas speculates on who might be criminally liable for

[24] Since the adoption of the Statute, the Appeals Chamber in the *Tadic* case, Judgment of 15 July 1999, para. 229, stated: 'The aider and abettor carries out acts specifically directed to assist, encourage or lend moral support to the perpetration of a certain specific crime (murder, extermination, rape, torture, wanton destruction of civilian property, etc.) and this support has a substantial effect upon the perpetration of the crime … In the case of aiding and abetting, the requisite mental element is knowledge that the acts performed by the aider and abettor assist the commission of a specific crime by the principal.' It remains to be seen to what extent this requirement that there be a substantial effect is taken up by the new International Criminal Court.

complicity in the international crimes recently committed in Sierra Leone:

> However, with regard to violations of international humanitarian law, establishing knowledge of the end use should generally be less difficult because of the scale and nature of the assistance. Given the intense publicity about war crimes and other atrocities in Sierra Leone, made known not only in specialised documents such as those issued by the United Nations and international non-governmental organisations but also by the popular media, a court ought to have little difficulty in concluding that diamond traders, airline pilots and executives, small arms suppliers and so on have knowledge of their contribution to the conflict and to the offences being committed.

> How far can the net be thrown? Assuming, for example, that the guilt of the diamond vendor who trades with combatants in Angola or Sierra Leone can actually be established, does liability extend to the merchant in Antwerp or Tel Aviv who purchases uncut stones knowing of their origin and that their sale is being used to help finance a rebel group guilty of atrocities? Why not? If we take this one step further, what of the bank manager of the diamond merchant who has purchased stones from a trader dealing with militias in Sierra Leone? If the bank manager is aware of the provenance of the funds, then he or she ought also to be held guilty as an accomplice. At this level of complicity, the knowledge

requirement is revived as the difficult part of the
case for the prosecution. Finally, what of the
young fiancé buying a low-cost diamond ring,
knowing plainly that the revenue will be funnelled
back to a terrorist army that chops the limbs off
little children? The further we go down the
complicity cascade, of course, the more difficult it
is to establish the 'substantial' nature of any
assistance, assuming this to be a requirement for
accomplice liability.[25]

Once we understand that individual criminal
complicity can extend so far into the structure and
networks that assist the principal perpetrators, repression and prosecution become much more a question of
political will than legal limitations.

But thinking about complicity does force all of us,
and especially those who are taking political decisions,
to consider how our actions affect the lives of others in
other countries. The prospect that, in light of the principles developed in Nuremberg, we may be liable for
prosecution in the International Criminal Court for
having facilitated an international crime ought to give
some people some reason to pause for thought.

The use of the complicity concept has, however, been

[25] W. Schabas, 'Enforcing International Humanitarian Law:
Catching the Accomplices' (2001) 83 *Review of the International
Committee of the Red Cross* 439–59 at 451.

taken in a further direction by human rights activists. Complicity is now sometimes used to suggest guilt through silence. This form of accusation has been extended beyond the traditional focus on governments and state agents and into the business world. The handbook, *Corporate Citizenship: Successful Strategies for Responsible Companies*, states:[26]

> It is not only governments that can stand accused of failing to uphold fundamental freedoms. Citizens, be they individuals or corporations, can also be complicit if they fail to acknowledge or take action on known violations …
>
> If corporations are citizens, from which we derive the concept of corporate citizenship, then they bear witness just as individuals do. If it is wrong for a person to turn away in the face of injustice, it is wrong for a corporation to do so. If you see your neighbor beating up another neighbor, do you do nothing? If a company operates in a country where there are systematic human rights violations, should the company remain silent?

This notion of silent complicity reflects the expectation on all authorities that they should take up human rights cases with the authorities. Indeed, it reflects the

[26] M. McIntosh, D. Leipziger, K. Jones and G. Coleman, *Corporate Citizenship: Successful Strategies for Responsible Companies* (Financial Times Pitman Publishing, London, 1998), p. 114.

growing acceptance by individuals and within companies that there is something culpable about failing to
exercise influence in such circumstances. The
Nuremberg trials made it clear that it was legitimate
under international law to take up questions relating to
the human rights of nationals mistreated by their
government. This in itself was a breakthrough. But the
modern human rights movement, and the way in which
it uses the notion of complicity, suggests that, not only
is it legitimate for governments to choose to protest and
prosecute, but that they also have a duty to act. Not only
do states have obligations to their nationals under international law, but governments also have duties towards
people in other countries. They have, in the words of
the recent report of the International Commission on
Intervention and State Sovereignty, a 'responsibility to
protect' individuals from violent attacks on their
human rights.[27] The Commission articulated the relevant basic principle as follows:

> Where a population is suffering serious harm, as a
> result of internal war, insurgency, repression or
> state failure, and the state in question is unwilling
> or unable to halt or avert it, the principle of non-

[27] International Commission on Intervention and State
Sovereignty, 'The Responsibility to Protect' (2001), available at
http://www.ciise-iciss.gc.ca/Report-English.asp.

> intervention yields to the international
> responsibility to protect.

Complaints of complicity respond to public promises of an ethical approach. I have sought to highlight here three dimensions of complicity in the current context. First, there is a growing sense of responsibility at the international level for human rights violations which go unpunished. This is especially so where powerful countries such as France or Britain do nothing to protect innocent civilians from rape, slaughter and humiliation. But it also extends down to our personal sense of morality and responsibility as we consider the impact of our actions as consumers, tourists, shareholders and investors. Secondly, in the period since the Nuremberg trial we have seen a determination to widen the net. International law is not only concerned with trials of the 'German major war criminals',[28] along with the 'leaders, organisers, instigators or accomplices' who conspired to have Japan wage wars of aggression.[29] International

[28] See *Goering et al.*, note 1 above.

[29] See the Judgment of the Tokyo Tribunal summarising count one of the indictment, at p. 48,421 of the original transcripts, reproduced in *The Tokyo War Crimes Trial: The Complete Transcripts of the Proceedings of the International Military Tribunal for the Far East in Twenty-Two Volumes* (annotated, compiled and edited by R. J. Pritchard and S. M. Zaide, Garland, New York and London, 1981), vol. 20, Judgment and Annexes.

criminal trials now stretch beyond the leaders, generals and ministers to reach right down to the camp commanders as well as into the commercial world, fixing on those who encourage and facilitate crimes. This widening of the net has come to embrace, at least at the level of accusation and expectation from non-governmental groups, a third dimension to the complicity concept. There is now an expectation that those with power, whether in the public or the private sector, have a duty to react to human rights violations where these fall within their 'sphere of influence'.[30] In this context, to do nothing is to be complicit. The increasing reliance on complicity as a central concept in human rights complaints reflects, in my view, an increased sense of solidarity with the victims of human rights abuses in other countries. It reflects a sense that the complainer recognises that there are now increased responsibilities which stretch across borders and that the bearers of those responsibilities are not simply a rarefied group of leaders. The responsibility extends to all of us.

[30] This phrase appears in the first principle of the UN's Global Compact, where the Secretary-General asked world business to 'support and respect the protection of internationally proclaimed human rights within their sphere of influence'. See generally A. Clapham, 'On Complicity', in M. Henzelin and R. Roth (eds.), *Le droit pénal à l'épreuve de l'internationalisation* (Georg and LGDI, Geneva and Paris, 2002), pp. 241–75 at pp. 243–6.

Complementarity

Let me finish with a few thoughts regarding the third connected concept of complementarity. This concept became an organising principle during the 1998 Rome Conference which drafted the Statute for the new International Criminal Court. In brief, it reflects the idea that priority must be given to trials for international crimes at the national level rather than at the new Court. Only if a state with jurisdiction is unable or unwilling to genuinely prosecute will the new Court be able to assert jurisdiction over the case. The Court is designed to complement national courts in a way which gives priority to national courts, where a state with jurisdiction wants to prosecute. For every defendant that comes before the Court, a state which would normally exercise jurisdiction will be able to demand that the international Prosecutor defer jurisdiction to that state. This deferral will happen unless a Trial Chamber decides pre-trial to authorise the investigation.

The new Court will not therefore operate like the other international courts I have mentioned. Nuremberg and Tokyo made few concessions to any demands from the states of Germany and Japan. The Yugoslavia and Rwanda Tribunals prioritise international trials. In the new system all nation states will be

able to demand exclusive jurisdiction for national prosecution before their own courts. Unlike the Nuremberg
and Tokyo Tribunals, the state of nationality of the
defendant will have a sort of priority over the new Court.
This principle is known (perhaps confusingly) as
complementarity.

At first sight, this probably seems like a huge defect in
the Statute. But it may be that the principle of complementarity will create a new international legal order. In
preparation for the entry into force of the Statute of the
International Criminal Court, dozens of states around
the world are considering national legislation to enable
them not only to surrender suspects to the new Court,
but also to assert jurisdiction over various categories of
individuals accused of genocide, crimes against humanity and war crimes. This is partly self-interested.
Without such legislation it may be impossible for a
government to reclaim a case for trial at the national
level. But the passage of such legislation has led to a
flurry of activity with regard to possible national trials
for war crimes and crimes against humanity. This is a
topic addressed by Professor Sands in his lecture in this
series.[31] Suffice it to say here that, as I speak, many
politicians now think twice before arranging their travel

[31] See chapter 3 below.

plans in case they find themselves in a state with appropriate complementary legislation to the Statute of the International Criminal Court. The complementarity at the heart of the Statute has generated a complementary transnational legal order for the prosecution of international crimes.

Conclusions

The concepts of complementarity, complicity and complexity were all central to the thinking of innovative physicists in the twentieth century. They served to help explain new ways of thinking about the physical and sub-atomic worlds as the traditional Newtonian understanding of physics gave way to a more complete understanding of the atomic world. These concepts were needed because existing notions failed to capture the new thinking and understanding. At their heart was the recognition that 'classical physics is just that idealisation in which we can speak about parts of the world without any reference to ourselves'.[32] The struggle to address international crimes and violations of human rights and humanitarian law is no longer something that we

[32] W. Heisenberg, *Physics and Philosophy* (Penguin Classics, London, 2000), pp. 22–3 (first published 1962).

are prepared to leave to others. Complementarity was used in part by physicists like Niels Bohr to explain the importance of how observation changes what we can measure about a particle. It introduces us to ourselves as essential factors in the search for knowledge and understanding. 'In this way quantum theory reminds us, as Bohr has put it, of the old wisdom that when searching for harmony in life one must never forget that in the drama of existence we are ourselves both players and spectators.'[33]

In closing, I would suggest that we too should be prepared for new ways of thinking about the prosecution of violations of international crimes. The Nuremberg model, based on victorious powers assuming jurisdiction over the losers, has given way to multilateral justice in the name of the whole international community acting through the Security Council. This was what happened with regard to the Tribunals established for the former Yugoslavia and Rwanda. On 1 July 2002, we entered a completely new era, where acts of genocide, crimes against humanity and war crimes all potentially fall under the jurisdiction of the new International Criminal Court established by more than eighty states parties. It is a fact that possible accomplices

[33] *Ibid.*, p. 25.

will include everyone, from the head of state, through the generals and soldiers right down to the mayors and even a supervisor in a tea factory. We can hope that this wide net of accountability, covering not only people in positions of authority but also those who simply aid and abet others, should serve to prevent crimes as people alter their conduct to avoid liability. The real story of the new Court may actually be the crimes which never take place. Just as Nuremberg served to educate a generation about the international commitment to repress war crimes and aggressive war, we can hope that the new Court in The Hague serves to put us all on notice that we all have responsibilities not only towards those we see around us but also those who suffer due to our action, our inaction and our silence.

3

After Pinochet: the role of national courts

PHILIPPE SANDS

Introduction

On 27 November 1998, a short letter was published in the *Guardian* newspaper in London. It read:

> The Cambodian couple in my street can't wait for Henry Kissinger's next visit.[1]

The letter was published two days after the landmark first decision of the Judicial Committee of the House of Lords, ruling that Senator Pinochet was not entitled to claim immunity from the jurisdiction of the English courts in respect of a Spanish extradition request to face criminal charges for torture and other crimes against humanity, while he was head of state in Chile.[2] The *Guardian* letter and the *Pinochet*

[1] *Guardian*, 27 November 1998, p. 25.

[2] *R. v. Bow Street Metropolitan Stipendiary Magistrate, ex parte Pinochet Ugarte* [2000] 1 AC 61 (House of Lords, Judgment, November 1998); also reported as *R. v. Bartle and the Commissioner of Police for the Metropolis, ex parte Pinochet*, (1998) 37 ILM 1302.

judgment were based on a theoretically simple – but politically explosive – premise: no rule of international law existed to prevent the arrest in London (whether for the purposes of prosecution before the English courts or for extradition to a third state) of an American or Chilean national for acts occurring outside the UK and involving no real connection with the territory or nationals of the UK.

The *Pinochet* judgment was a landmark because it emphasised the role of national courts – Spanish and English – for the prosecution of the most serious international crimes. It relied on three principles:

1. that there are certain crimes that are so serious that they are treated by the international community as being international crimes over which any state may, in principle, claim jurisdiction;
2. that national courts, rather than just international courts, can – and in some cases must – exercise jurisdiction over these international crimes, irrespective of any direct connection with the acts; and
3. that in respect of these crimes it can no longer be assumed that immunities will be accorded to former sovereigns or high officials.

The emergence of these principles is closely connected to the proceedings at the Nuremberg and

Tokyo war crimes tribunals, addressed by Professors Clapham and Overy in their lectures. In his lecture, Professor Clapham addressed the contribution which the Nuremberg proceedings have made to the subsequent development of international law.[3] He described the way in which the substantive norms of international law – both international human rights law and international humanitarian law – have been influenced by the emergent principles which the Nuremberg judges developed and applied. He described the complexities of the law; the prospects and challenges of the emerging principles governing liability for complicity in war crimes, crimes against humanity and genocide; and he concluded by touching on the principle of 'complementarity', that is to say, the relationship between national courts and international courts in the exercise of jurisdiction over the most serious crimes.

I address some of the issues which arise when we ask the general question: which courts – national or international – are best suited to exercise jurisdiction over individuals accused of crimes against humanity, war crimes and genocide? In posing that question, I should state at the outset that I proceed on the basis that criminal justice

---

[3]   See chapter 2 above.

dispensed through courts (national or international) can be an appropriate way – although not the only way – of dealing with the most serious international crimes. That is not an assumption which is universally held, as a growing literature on the subject indicates. Criminal law in general – and international law in particular – will never be a panacea for the ills of the world. And there are other means for dealing with the gravest crimes: they can be ignored; they can be the subject of national amnesties; they can be addressed through processes which have come to be known as 'truth and reconciliation'; they can be the subject of extra-judicial means providing for summary justice; and they can be the subject of diplomatic deals.

But, for better or worse, and whatever theoretical or policy justifications may be found (whether deterrence, or punishment, or the 'seeking of the truth'), the international community has determined that the gravest crimes are properly the subject of criminal justice systems. If nothing else, that is one clear consequence of the creation of the International Criminal Court:[4] in establishing it, the international community has determined that criminal courts (as opposed to civil courts, or administrative courts, or human rights courts) are to be

[4] Statute of the International Criminal Court, Rome, 17 July 1998, in force 2 July 2002, (1999) 37 ILM 999.

a principal means for the enforcement of international criminal law, and that national courts (within the state in which the crimes are committed and in third states) and international courts have a role to play.

In recent years, national courts have become more prominent in these matters. They are faced with different circumstances. In most situations, national courts will deal with cases relating to facts which have occurred within the geographical area in which they are located. But it has become clear that national courts will only rarely try their own nationals where war crimes are concerned, and even more rarely where crimes against humanity or genocide are concerned. In some cases, national proceedings are concerned with acts occurring outside the state seeking to exercise jurisdiction, when the sole connection is the presence of the defendant within the geographical jurisdiction of the state. That was the *Pinochet* case,[5] and the case against Hissene Habré in Senegal.[6] In other cases, indictments have been issued when the defendant is not even present in the jurisdiction: that is the case for the indictment by a

---

[5]   *R. v. Bow Street Metropolitan Stipendiary Magistrate, ex parte Pinochet Ugarte (No. 3)* [2000] 1 AC 147.

[6]   *Cour de Cassation* (Senegal's Court of Final Appeals), judgment of 20 March 2001, which upheld the Court of Appeal's decision to dismiss the charges.

Belgian prosecutor of Prime Minister Sharon[7] and of a foreign minister of Congo,[8] a case to which I shall return, as well as the proceedings against President Gaddafi in France.[9] And states have been creative in finding other means: the Lockerbie proceedings in a Scottish criminal court (and then an appeals court) relocated to the Netherlands.[10] And internationalised national courts are established or being established to

[7] *The Complaint Against Ariel Sharon,* Cour d'Appel de Bruxelles, Chambre des Mises en Accusation, Pen. 1632/01, judgment of 26 June 2002.

[8] *Democratic Republic of the Congo v. Belgium, Case Concerning the Arrest Warrant of 11 April 2000,* ICJ, General List No. 121, judgment of 14 February 2002, www.icj-cij.org/icjwww/idocket/iCOBE/icobejudgment/icobe_ijudgment_20020214.pdf.

[9] *Arret, Cour de Cassation,* 13 March 2001, No. 1414. See also *Arret, Cour d'Appel de Paris – Chambre d'accusation,* 20 October 2000, www.sos-attentats.org. For a discussion of this case, see Salvatore Zappala, 'Do Heads of State in Office Enjoy Immunity from Jurisdiction for International Crimes? The Ghaddafi Case Before the French Cour de Cassation' (2001) 12 *European Journal of International Law* 595–612.

[10] *Her Majesty's Advocate v. Megrahi,* No. 1475/99, High Court of Justiciary at Camp Zeist (Kamp van Zeist), 31 January 2001, www.scotcourts.gov.uk/index1.asp. See also Omer Y. Elagab, 'The Hague as the Seat of the Lockerbie Trial: Some Constraints' (2000) 34 *International Lawyer* 289–306; Sean D. Murphy, 'Contemporary Practice of the United States Relating to International Law: Verdict in the Trial of the Lockerbie Bombing Suspects' (2001) 95 *American Journal of International Law* 405–7.

deal with international crimes in Bosnia, in East Timor, in Sierra Leone and in Cambodia.[11]

Against this background I will explore the relationship between national criminal courts and international criminal courts. The international community has determined that both should play a role in combating impunity.

The International Criminal Court

It is appropriate to begin with the International Criminal Court (ICC). The Statute emphasises 'that the ICC established under this Statute shall be *complementary* to national criminal jurisdictions'.[12] The Statute thus gives effect to what is now referred to as the 'principle of complementarity'. This means that the ICC will not be entitled to exercise jurisdiction if the case is

[11] See e.g. the following articles for a discussion of these proposals: Robert Cryer, 'A "Special Court" for Sierra Leone?' (2001) 50 *International and Comparative Law Quarterly* 435–46; and Boris Kondoch, 'The United Nations Administration of East Timor' (2001) 6 *Journal of Conflict and Security Law* 245–65. For a discussion of international courts in general, see Cesare P. R. Romano, 'The Proliferation of International Judicial Bodies: The Pieces of the Puzzle' (1999) 31 *New York University Journal of International Law and Politics* 709.

[12] Note 4 above, Preamble (emphasis added).

being investigated or prosecuted by a state which has jurisdiction over it, or if the case has been investigated by a state which has jurisdiction over it and the state has decided not to prosecute for genuine reasons, or if the person has already been tried for conduct which is the subject of the complaint 'by another court'.[13] The 'principle of complementarity' means that, in the emerging institutional architecture of international criminal justice, the jurisdiction of the ICC will not be hierarchically superior to that of national courts. Indeed, the ICC Statute gives primacy to national courts. This reflects a desire to maintain a degree of respect for traditional sovereignty. It means that it will be first and foremost for these courts to act; the ICC will play a residual role, serving as a long-stop in the event that justice is inadequately dispensed at the national level.

The policy here being applied is not an accidental one, but rather the product of deliberation and negotiations carried on over many years. The international community is saying that it is primarily for national courts to exercise jurisdiction. There are several rationales for that policy: (1) it recognises that national courts will often be the best placed to deal with international crimes, taking into account the availability of

---

[13] *Ibid.*, Articles 17(1)(a), (b) and (c) and 20(3).

evidence and witnesses, and cost factors; (2) it recognises that the human and financial burdens of exercising criminal justice have to be spread around, they cannot be centralised in The Hague; (3) it creates an incentive for states, to encourage them to develop and then apply their national criminal justice systems as a way of avoiding the exercise of jurisdiction by the ICC; and (4) in the expectation that that will happen, it might allow more states to become parties to the ICC Statute, reassured in the knowledge that they have it within their own power to determine whether or not the ICC will exercise jurisdiction.

In contrast to other signatory states, including the United Kingdom, the United States is not reassured that politically motivated or malicious prosecutions will not be brought before the ICC.[14] Even though the ICC will adjudicate only the most serious international crimes where national courts are unable to act, and these crimes are defined in accordance with the United States' own Code of Military Justice,[15] the US has sought to ensure that its peacekeepers would be permanently

[14] On some of the US arguments, see Philippe Sands, 'The Future of International Adjudication' (1999) 14 *Connecticut Journal of International Law* 1–13.

[15] Uniform Code of Military Justice, 10 USC 801–941; also in Manual for Courts-Martial, United States, Appendix 2, at A2-1 to A2-35 (2000).

exempted from the ICC's jurisdiction. This proposal has been rejected by the United Nations Security Council, in favour of a year-long immunity, which may or may not be renewed.

It should be mentioned that the primacy accorded by the ICC Statute to national courts has not been the governing principle for other international courts. The Statutes of the International Criminal Tribunals for Rwanda (ICTR)[16] and for the former Yugoslavia (ICTY)[17] recognise the concurrent jurisdiction of national courts in Rwanda and the former Yugoslavia in relation to the crimes over which those two international criminal tribunals have jurisdiction. In both cases, however, the tribunals will have primacy if they so decide.[18] Each Tribunal's Statute provides that: 'At any

[16] UN Security Council Resolution 955, (1994) 33 ILM 1598.

[17] Contained within the 'Secretary-General's Report on Aspects of Establishing an International Tribunal for the Prosecution of Persons Responsible for Serious Violations of International Humanitarian Law Committed in the Territory of the Former Yugoslavia' (1993) 32 ILM 1159; adopted by UN Security Council Resolution 827 (1993), (1993) 32 ILM 1203.

[18] Article 9 of the ICTY Statute provides:
  1. The International Tribunal and national courts shall have concurrent jurisdiction to prosecute persons for serious violations of international humanitarian law committed in the territory of the former Yugoslavia since 1 January 1991.
  2. The International Tribunal shall have primacy over national courts. At any stage of the procedure, the International Tribunal may formally request national courts to defer to the competence of the International Tribunal in accordance

stage of the procedure, the International Tribunal may formally request national courts to defer to the competence of the International Tribunal in accordance with [its] Statute and the Rules of Procedure and Evidence.'[19] That primacy has been challenged. In the *Tadic* case, for example, the defendant argued that the primacy of the ICTY violated the domestic jurisdiction of states and their sovereignty. The Appeal Chamber rejected the claim. It said:

> When an international tribunal such as the present one is created, it must be endowed with primacy over national courts. Otherwise, human nature

with the present Statute and the Rules of Procedure and Evidence of the International Tribunal.

Article 8 of the ICTR Statute provides:

1. The International Tribunal for Rwanda and national courts shall have concurrent jurisdiction to prosecute persons for serious violations of international humanitarian law committed in the territory of Rwanda and Rwandan citizens for such violations committed in the territory of neighbouring States, between 1 January 1994 and 31 December 1994.

2. The International Tribunal for Rwanda shall have primacy over the national courts of all States. At any stage of the procedure, the International Tribunal for Rwanda may formally request national courts to defer to its competence in accordance with the present Statute and the Rules of Procedure and Evidence of the International Tribunal for Rwanda.

See Bartram Brown, 'Primacy or Complementarity: Reconciling the Jurisdiction of National Courts and International Criminal Tribunals' (1998) 23 *Yale Journal of International Law* 383 at 386.

19 *Ibid.*

being what it is, there would be a perennial danger
of international crimes being characterised as
'ordinary crimes' or proceedings being 'designed to
shield the accused', or cases not being diligently
prosecuted. If not effectively countered by the
principle of primacy, any one of those stratagems
might be used to defeat the very purpose of the
creation of an international criminal jurisdiction,
to the benefit of the very people whom it has been
designed to prosecute.[20]

The Constitution of the Nuremberg Tribunal did not
address the relationship with national courts. However,
it established the right of the competent authority of
any signatory of the Constitution to bring individuals
to trial for membership of criminal groups or organisations, before national, military or occupation courts.[21]
In such cases, it stated that 'the criminal nature of the
group or organisation is considered proved and shall
not be questioned'.[22] The only function for the national

---

20 *Prosecutor* v. *Tadic*, Case No IT-94-1, Decision on the Defence
Motion for Interlocutory Appeal on Jurisdiction, 2 October
1995, paras. 58–9, www.un.org/icty/ind-e.htm; Tadic: Appeals
Chamber Decisions.
21 Charter of the International Military Tribunal, Part I,
'Constitution of the International Military Tribunal', Article 10,
annexed to the London Agreement for the Prosecution and
Punishment of the Major War Criminals of the European Axis,
London, 8 August 1945.
22 *Ibid.*

courts was in relation to membership of a criminal organisation. It also provided that any person convicted by the Tribunal could also be charged before national, military or occupation courts with a crime other than membership in a criminal group or organisation.[23] The Constitution of the Nuremberg Tribunal also allowed proceedings against a person in his absence.[24] There was no question that national courts would have a concurrent jurisdiction, let alone primacy.

In summary, the constituent instruments of these various international courts and tribunals indicate the trend towards a greater role for national courts: at Nuremberg and Tokyo, the international jurisdictions were exclusive, and even established the jurisdiction of the national courts; in the case of Rwanda and Yugoslavia, the exercise of international jurisdiction is concurrent with the jurisdiction of the local courts, but the international courts have primacy; the new ICC, however, will only have a residual jurisdiction and will not be able to trump the proper exercise of national criminal jurisdiction, assuming it has been properly exercised. The ICC will have primacy, however, in determining whether or not a national prosecution has been properly carried out.

[23] *Ibid.*, Article 11.
[24] *Ibid.*, Article 12.

There are obviously good reasons for preferring national courts to international courts, particularly if the courts are in the state in which the criminal acts occurred. The evidence – and the witnesses – are likely to be more easily accessible, at least in a geographical sense, and that will make the criminal justice process more cost-effective. But when one talks about national courts one is no longer considering only the courts of the state in which the acts occurred. 'National courts' also means other national courts, in states which may have only a limited connection with the crime – perhaps because the perpetrator or the victim is a national of another state, or the perpetrator happens to be present in another state. In those situations, the logic behind the grant of jurisdiction is not based on considerations of cost or access to evidence, but relates to the connection between a state and its own nationals. The principle that a state may exercise 'long-arm' criminal jurisdiction over its own nationals is well established. What is more recent is the idea that certain crimes are so horrendous that the international community has determined that any state is entitled to exercise jurisdiction over them, in the quest to avoid impunity.

International law promotes a role for national courts

The general principle has been that states only exercise criminal jurisdiction over offences which occur within their geographical boundaries. However, that has changed, as the House of Lords recognised in *Pinochet No. 3*:

> Since the Nazi atrocities and the Nuremberg trials, international law has recognised a number of offences as being international crimes. Individual states have taken jurisdiction to try some international crimes even in cases where such crimes were not committed within the geographical boundaries of such states.[25]

Until 1945, the rules of public international law were very limited. There were rules governing the methods and means of warfare, which among other things established protections for civilians. And there were rules governing the treatment of aliens (non-nationals). But there were no international treaties and conventions establishing minimum standards of human rights to place limits on what a state could do or permit to be

---

25 *R.* v. *Bow Street Metropolitan Stipendiary Magistrate, ex parte Pinochet Ugarte (No. 3)* [2000] 1 AC 147 at 189 *per* Lord Browne-Wilkinson.

done to its own people. There was no clearly articulated international rule of law prohibiting the most serious crimes, such as genocide, torture or the disappearance of people. Article 6 of the Constitution of the Nuremberg Tribunal was of singular importance because it restated the crimes over which the Tribunal would have jurisdiction, and in so doing effectively set down a code.[26] It had jurisdiction over crimes against peace, war crimes and crimes against humanity. As Lord Browne-Wilkinson put it:

> Although there may be legitimate doubts as to the legality of the Nuremberg Charter … in my judgment those doubts were stilled by the Affirmation of the Principles of International Law recognised by the Charter of the Nuremberg Tribunal adopted by the United Nations General Assembly on 11 December 1946.[27] That affirmation affirmed the principles of international law recognised by the Charter of the Nuremberg Tribunal and the judgment of the tribunal and directed the committee on the codification of international law to treat as a matter of primary importance plans for the formulation of the principles recognised in the Charter of the Nuremberg Tribunal. At least from that date

[26] Charter of the International Military Tribunal, note 21 above, Article 6.
[27] General Assembly Resolution 95, 1st Sess., 1144; UN Doc. A/236 (1946).

> onwards the concept of personal liability for a
> crime in international law must have been part of
> international law.[28]

In the period after Nuremberg, the United Nations Charter provided a forum for the adoption of new international conventions which would flesh out more detailed rules criminalising these acts. These rules were developed in the framework of an international legal order in which there was no international criminal court. The enforcement of the rules would have to be a matter for national courts.

In 1948, the United Nations General Assembly promulgated the first of several instruments which the International Court of Justice in The Hague has recently characterised as reflecting an 'extension of jurisdiction',[29] namely the 1948 Convention on the Prevention and Punishment of the Crime of Genocide.[30] Article I of the 1948 Convention confirmed that genocide was 'a crime under international law' which the parties undertook to prevent and punish.[31] The fourth 1949 Geneva

---

[28] *R. v. Bow Street Metropolitan Stipendiary Magistrate, ex parte Pinochet Ugarte (No. 3)* [2000] 1 AC 147 at 197 *per* Lord Browne-Wilkinson.

[29] *Congo* v. *Belgium*, note 8 above, para. 59.

[30] 78 UNTS 277; Annex to General Assembly Resolution 260-A (III) of 9 December 1948.

[31] *Ibid.*, Article I.

Convention established protections for civilians in times of war.[32] A 1973 convention declared that apartheid was a crime against humanity.[33] A 1979 convention criminalised the taking of hostages. A 1984 convention committed parties to take effective measures to prevent acts of torture in any territory under their jurisdiction.[34] These instruments did not merely criminalise the acts which they addressed. They committed their parties to take judicial measures to prevent and to punish these crimes. And they did so in broadly similar ways. Article VI of the 1948 Genocide Convention states:

> Persons charged with genocide or any of the other acts enumerated in [the Convention] shall be tried by a competent tribunal of the State in the territory of which the act was committed, or by such international penal tribunal as may have jurisdiction with respect to those Contracting Parties which shall have accepted its jurisdiction.[35]

[32] Geneva Convention Relative to the Protection of Civilian Persons in Time of War (Geneva IV), (1950) 75 UNTS 287–417.

[33] International Convention on the Suppression and Punishment of the Crime of Apartheid, adopted 30 November 1973, 1015 UNTS 243; Annex to General Assembly Resolution 3068 (XXVIII).

[34] Convention Against Torture and Other Cruel, Inhuman or Degrading Treatment or Punishment, adopted 10 December 1984, General Assembly Resolution 39/46, 39 UN GAOR Supp. (No. 51) at 197, UN Doc. A/39/51 (1985); (1984) 23 ILM 1027; substantive changes noted in (1985) 24 ILM 535.

[35] Note 30 above, Article VI.

In this provision we see, for the first time, a commitment to prevent impunity reflected in the obligation to prosecute before national criminal courts (although it is limited to such acts as occurred in the territory of the state), but without expressly limiting the right to states to exercise a more extensive jurisdiction. The 1949 Geneva Convention on the protection of civilians went a step further. It too commits parties to enact 'any legislation necessary to provide effective penal sanctions for committing, or ordering to be committed ... grave breaches of the ... Convention'.[36] But it then goes on to establish a further obligation, a positive obligation on parties to:

> search for persons alleged to have committed, or to have ordered to be committed, such grave breaches, and shall bring such persons, regardless of their nationality, before its own courts. It may also, if it prefers, and in accordance with the provisions of its own legislation, hand such persons over for trial to another [party] concerned, provided such [party] has made out a *prima facie* case.[37]

The difference between the 1948 Genocide Convention and the 1949 Geneva Convention is that, in the latter, there is no geographical limitation: the obligation to

---

[36] Note 32 above, Article 146.
[37] *Ibid.*

prosecute is not limited to acts which occur within the territory of the state required to prosecute. So if a person commits a grave violation of the 1949 Convention – for example, wilful killing or torture of a civilian – in France and is then discovered to be in the United Kingdom by the relevant authorities, he or she must be 'searched for' and brought before the English courts or handed over to another concerned party, for example France. The commitment to root out impunity is extended to what has come to be known as 'universal criminal jurisdiction': the right of states to exercise national jurisdiction over a criminal act irrespective of where it occurred. This is not a new development – international law had long recognised universal jurisdiction for piracy and slavery, for example – but it marks an extension of the principle, in a modified form, into a new subject area.

The same commitment is to be found in other international conventions subsequently adopted. For example, the 1973 Apartheid Convention provides that a person charged with the crime of apartheid may be tried 'by a competent tribunal of any state party to the Convention which may acquire jurisdiction of the person of the accused'.[38]

---

[38] Note 33 above, Article V. Note that the language is 'may' rather than 'shall'. International penal tribunals may also exercise jurisdiction.

The further development of this broad, universalis-
ing approach is to be found in the 1984 Torture
Convention, which came to assume singular importance in the proceedings involving Senator Pinochet.
The Convention requires parties to establish jurisdiction over offences of torture when the offence is
committed in its territory, when the alleged offender is
one of its own nationals, or when the victim is one of its
nationals if it considers it appropriate.[39] It also requires
the parties to establish jurisdiction over Convention
offences 'in cases where the alleged offender is present
in any territory under its jurisdiction and it does not
extradite him'.[40] In relation to each of these cases, the
parties must prosecute or extradite all such persons.[41]
The principle behind the approach is clear: there is to be
no impunity for torturers, wherever they may be found.
Messrs Burgers and Danelius (the former was the chair-
man of the United Nations Working Group on the
Torture Convention, and both were draftsmen of its
first draft) say in their authoritative *Handbook on the
Convention Against Torture and Other Cruel, Inhuman
or Degrading Treatment or Punishment* that it was 'an
essential purpose [of the convention] to ensure that a

[39]   Note 34 above, Article 5(1).
[40]   *Ibid.*, Article 5(2).
[41]   *Ibid.*, Article 7(1).

torturer does not escape the consequences of his acts by going to another country'.[42]

These instruments were adopted in the absence of any international criminal court. They confirm the commitment of the international community to criminalise certain acts and to impose the obligation to prosecute before national courts individuals who are alleged to have committed the criminalised acts. The promotion of national jurisdictions is consistent with the trend I have described earlier, which promotes the ICC as a court of last resort.

Pinochet

Senator Pinochet was arrested on 16 October 1998. He made an immediate application for *habeas corpus*, on the ground that, as a former head of state, he was entitled to immunity from the jurisdiction of the English courts. The basis for that argument was reflected in classical principles of international law, going back over a century, for example the decision of 1876 of the State Supreme Court

---

[42] Herman Burgers and Hans Danelius, *The United Nations Convention Against Torture: A Handbook on the Convention Against Torture and Other Cruel, Inhuman or Degrading Treatment or Punishment* (1988), p. 131.

of New York in *Hatch* v. *Baez*.[43] That court was faced with a claim from a plaintiff, Mr Davis Hatch, that he had suffered injuries in the Dominican Republic as a result of acts done by the defendant, Mr Buenaventura Baez, in his official capacity of President of the Dominican Republic. When Mr Hatch learnt that former President Baez was present in New York he brought proceedings. The court found that it could in principle exercise jurisdiction, given the defendant's presence in New York. But it ruled in favour of the defendant's claim to immunity from its jurisdiction on the grounds that such immunity was 'essential to preserve the peace and harmony of nations', because the acts alleged sprang from the capacity in which the acts were done, and because they emanated from a foreign and friendly government.[44] The decision was unexceptional, based on a traditional judicial respect for the sovereignty of a foreign state.

The approach reflected in the 1876 decision was broadly followed by the court of first instance in the *Pinochet* case, which upheld Senator Pinochet's claim to immunity.[45] On appeal to the House of Lords in November 1998, however, that ruling was overturned by

43 *Hatch* v. *Baez*, 7 Hun 596 (NY 1876).

44 *Ibid.*, p. 600.

45 *Re Augusto Pinochet Ugarte*, UK High Court of Justice, Queen's Bench Division (Divisional Court), 28 October 1998, (1999) 38 ILM 68.

three votes to two, on the ground that customary international law provided no basis to uphold the claim to immunity.[46] The significance of the ruling was evident from the fact that it made front-page news around the world, most of which was positive.[47] That judgment of the House of Lords was later annulled for other reasons,

[46] *R. v. Bow Street Metropolitan Stipendiary Magistrate, ex parte Pinochet Ugarte* [2000] 1 AC 61.

[47] For an example of the reaction in the press, see Warren Hoge, 'British Court Rules Against Pinochet: Now Cabinet Must Weigh Extradition', *New York Times*, 26 November 1998, p. A1; Kenneth Roth, 'Justice for Tyrants', *Washington Post*, 26 November 1998, p. A31; 'Pinochet: le Jour où la Peur a Changé de Camp', *Le Monde* (Paris), 27 November 1998, p. 1; Guy Duplat, 'Un début de Justice', *Le Soir* (Brussels), 26 November 1998, p. 1; Nick Hopkins and Jamie Wilson, 'Judgment Day Beckons', *Guardian* (London), 26 November 1998, p. 1; Paola Sais, 'Pinochet sin immunidad', *La Tercera* (Santiago, Chile), 26 November 1998; and 'Un hito en la defensa de los derechos humanos', *El Mundo* (Madrid), 26 November 1998. See also the numerous subsequent law review articles, for example, Michael Byers, 'The Law and Politics of the Pinochet Case' (2000) 10 *Duke Journal of Comparative and International Law* 415, available at www.law.duke.edu/journals/djcil/articles/djcil10p415. htm; Roland Bank, 'Der Fall Pinochet: Aufbruch zu neuen Ufern bei der Verfolgung von Menschenrechtsverletzungen?' (1999) 59 *Zeitschrift fum ur auslum andisches um offentliches Recht und Vum olkerrecht* 677; Andrea Bianchi, 'Immunity Versus Human Rights: The Pinochet Case' (1999) 10 *European Journal of International Law* 237; Neil Boister and Richard Burchill, 'The Implications of the Pinochet Decisions for the Extradition or Prosecution of Former South African Heads of State for Crimes Committed Under Apartheid' (1999) 11 *African Journal of International and Comparative Law* 619; Michel Cosnard, 'Quelques Observations Sur les Décisions de

but there followed a further judgment which made a
similar finding, although on narrower grounds, namely,
that the loss of immunity arose not under customary
international law, but rather from the coming into force
in late 1988 of the 1984 Convention Against Torture,[48] to
which Chile, Spain and the United Kingdom were all
parties.[49] The fact that the majority of the House of Lords

la Chambre des Lords du 25 novembre 1998 et du 24 mars 1999
dans l'Affaire Pinochet' (1999) 103 *Revue Générale de Droit
International Public* 309; Hazel Fox, 'The First Pinochet Case:
Immunity of a Former Head of State' (1999) 48 *International and
Comparative Law Quarterly* 207; and Jill M. Sears, 'Confronting
the "Culture of Impunity": Immunity of Heads of State from
Nuremberg to Ex parte Pinochet' (1999) 42 *German Yearbook of
International Law* 125.

[48] Note 34 above. For more information on the Convention, see
Herman Burgers and Hans Danelius, *The United Nations
Convention Against Torture: A Handbook on the Convention
Against Torture and Other Cruel, Inhuman, or Degrading
Treatment or Punishment* (1988); Roland Bank, *Die interna-
tionale Bekum ampfung von Folter und unmenschlicher
Behandlung auf den Ebenen der Vereinten Nationen und des
Europates: eine vergleichende Analyse von Implementation und
Effektivitum at der neueren Kontrollmechanismen* (1996); and
Roland Bank, 'International Efforts to Combat Torture and
Inhuman Treatment: Have the New Mechanisms Improved
Protection?' (1997) 8 *European Journal of International Law* 613.

[49] Chile became a party on 30 September 1988; Spain became a
party on 21 October 1989; the United Kingdom became a party
on 8 December 1988. See United Nations, 'Status of Multilateral
Treaties Deposited with the Secretary-General', at http://
untreaty.un.org/english/bible/englishinternetbible/partI/chapt
erIV/treaty12.asp.

relied on the 1984 Convention indicated a desire to respect state sovereignty as expressed through the consent to be bound by the Convention; the difficulty with this approach, as Lord Goff recognised in his lone dissent, was that the 1984 Convention was silent about immunity, and on that basis a loss of immunity could not be presumed.[50] But Lord Goff was unable to persuade his fellow judges to take the traditional approach, and six of the seven Law Lords ruled against the claim to immunity.

The ruling of the House of Lords was a landmark, and has been recognised as such. First, the majority judgments recognised the legitimate role which national courts are to play in the prosecution of those international crimes which are outlawed by instruments such as the Torture Convention and the other conventions mentioned earlier in this lecture. Secondly, it recognised and gave effect to the underlying policy of those conventions, which establishes the principle of universal jurisdiction over such crimes. Thirdly, it recognised that the grant of immunity to a former head of state would be incompatible with the objectives of the Torture Convention, and that a proper interpretation of the Convention required a rejection of immunity. And, fourthly, it underscored the point that the

---

[50] *R. v. Bow Street Metropolitan Stipendiary Magistrate, ex parte Pinochet Ugarte (No. 3)* [2000] 1 AC 147 at 215 *per* Lord Goff.

commission of an international crime can never be an official function. As Lord Browne-Wilkinson put it:

> Can it be said that the commission of a crime which is an international crime against humanity and *jus cogens* is an act done in an official capacity on behalf of the state? I believe there to be strong ground for saying that the implementation of torture as defined by the Torture Convention cannot be a state function.[51]

And Lord Phillips was unable to identify a rule of immunity upon which Senator Pinochet could rely:

> I reach that conclusion on the simple basis that no established rule of international law requires state immunity *ratione materiae* to be accorded in respect of prosecution for an international crime. International crimes and extra-territorial jurisdiction in relation to them are both new arrivals in the field of public international law. I do not believe that state immunity *ratione materiae* can co-exist with them. The exercise of extra-territorial jurisdiction overrides the principle that one state will not intervene in the internal affairs of another. It does so because, where international crime is concerned, that principle cannot prevail. An international crime is as offensive, if not more offensive, to the international community when committed under colour of office. Once extra-territorial jurisdiction is established, it makes no

[51] *Ibid.*, p. 203 *per* Lord Browne-Wilkinson.

sense to exclude from it acts done in an official capacity.[52]

The judgment of the House of Lords opens the door to the use of a national court to prosecute an individual – even a former head of state – for acts occurring in another state. It provides strong support for the potential role of national courts, against the background of the principle of 'complementarity' found in the Statute of the ICC. But the judgment of the House of Lords has also given rise to a vibrant debate on the circumstances in which jurisdiction of a national court may be claimed and then exercised. There is, in particular, concern that inroads into the traditional immunities of foreign sovereigns might undermine the ability of states to interact, especially where traditional immunities are challenged in respect of serving heads of state or other officials.

The World Court steps in

Our story now turns away from a national court to another international court in The Hague, the International Court of Justice (the ICJ, sometimes

[52] *Ibid.*, p. 289 *per* Lord Phillips.

known as the 'World Court'), which is the principal judicial organ of the United Nations. The question of immunity before national courts for international crimes was addressed by the ICJ in the recent case of *Congo* v. *Belgium*.[53]

On 11 April 2000, a Belgian investigating judge issued an international arrest warrant against the serving Minister of Foreign Affairs of the Democratic Republic of Congo, Mr Abdualye Yerodia Ndombasi. The arrest warrant was served *in absentia*. The arrest warrant accused Mr Yerodia of making various speeches in August 1998 inciting racial hatred. It alleged that the speeches had the effect of inciting the population to attack Tutsi residents in Kinshasa, which resulted in several hundred deaths, lynchings, internments, summary executions and arbitrary arrests and unfair trials. He was charged with crimes under Belgian law concerning the punishment of grave breaches of the Geneva Convention of 1949 and their Additional Protocols I and II of 1977 and the punishment of serious violation of international humanitarian law. The relevant Belgian law provided that its courts would have jurisdiction in respect of offences committed anywhere in the world (absolute universal jurisdiction). And it provided that no person would be able to claim immunity from the jurisdiction of the

[53] *Congo* v. *Belgium*, note 8 above.

Belgian courts.[54] In sum, Belgium was purporting to exercise jurisdiction over acts which had taken place outside Belgium, involving no Belgian citizens, and without Mr Yerodia being present in Belgium.

One can understand the motivations of the Belgian prosecuting judge, but also those of the Congo. In October 2000, the Congo brought proceedings before the ICJ in The Hague, calling on the Court to take steps to require Belgium to annul the arrest warrant. In its application, the Congo asserted that the purported claim to be able to exercise universal jurisdiction violated the sovereignty of the Congo, and that the non-recognition of the immunity of a serving foreign minister violated international law concerning diplomatic immunities. The Court decided that it was not required to address the first question, concerning the circumstances in which a state may exercise universal jurisdiction.[55] On the question of immunities, the Court ruled that the matter fell to be

---

[54] Law of 16 June 1993 Concerning Punishment of Grave Breaches of the International Geneva Conventions of 12 August 1949 and of Protocols I and II of 8 June 1977 Additional Thereto, as amended by the Law of 19 February 1999 Concerning Punishment of Serious Violations of International Humanitarian Law, *Moniteur belge*, 5 August 1993, *Moniteur belge*, 23 March 1999, Articles 7 and 5(3).

[55] It may be that the trenchant criticism of the idea of universal jurisdiction found in the Separate Opinion of the President of the Court, Judge Guillaume, did not find favour with a majority

governed by customary international law, since the relevant treaties contained no provision 'specifically defining the immunities enjoyed by Ministers for Foreign Affairs'.[56] The Court found that, as a matter of principle, 'the functions of a Minister of Foreign Affairs are such that, throughout the duration of his or her office, he or she when abroad enjoys full immunity from criminal jurisdiction and inviolability'.[57] The Court provided no judicial, academic or other authority to support its conclusion. It then considered whether such immunities could be claimed where the Minister is suspected of having committed war crimes or crimes against humanity (and one might add genocide). It found – on the basis of a careful examination of state practice – that it was unable 'to deduce from this practice that there exists under customary international law any form of exception to the rule according immunity from criminal jurisdiction and inviolability to incumbent Ministers for Foreign Affairs, where they are suspected of having committed war crimes or crime against humanity'.[58] The rules of the various international criminal tribunals,

of the judges: *Congo* v. *Belgium*, note 8 above, Separate Opinion of Guillame, paras. 4–12 and 16, available at www.icj-cij.org/ icjwww/idocket/iCOBE/icobejudgment/icobe_ijudgment_20020214_guillaume.pdf.

[56] *Congo* v. *Belgium*, note 8 above, para. 52.
[57] *Ibid.*, para. 54.   [58] *Ibid.*, para. 58.

including those of the ICC, which dispense with immunity, did not alter its conclusion.[59] Nor did international conventions establishing jurisdiction, but silent on the question of immunities. The reasoning of the ICJ is thin, to say the least.

The Court appears to have been concerned about the message which would be conveyed by its judgment. It pointed out that immunity from jurisdiction was not the same thing as impunity in respect of crimes, including the most serious crimes. It identified four available options for the prosecution of international criminals.

First, the ICJ noted that they could be tried by the national courts of their own country, since international law provided no immunities in such circumstances. Experience tells us that this option is almost entirely theoretical. I cannot put it more succinctly than Lord Browne-Wilkinson:

> [T]he fact that the local court had jurisdiction to deal with the international crime of torture was nothing to the point so long as the totalitarian regime remained in power: a totalitarian regime will not permit adjudication by its own courts on

[59] See Charter of the International Military Tribunals at Nuremberg, Article 7; Charter of the International Military Tribunal for the Far East, Article 6; Statute of the International Criminal Tribunal for the former Yugoslavia, Article 7(2); Statute of the International Criminal Tribunal for Rwanda, Article 6(2); and Statute of the International Criminal Court, Article 27.

> its own shortcomings. Hence the demand for some
> international machinery to repress state torture
> which is not dependent upon the local courts where
> the torture was committed.[60]

Secondly, the ICJ considered that the state which they represent or have represented could waive immunity. Again, it is difficult to see the circumstances in which a state will waive immunity for a serving foreign minister. Several actions brought against the former Philippine President, Ferdinand Marcos, during the late 1980s are an exception; in *In Re Grand Jury Proceedings*,[61] Marcos' immunity was waived by the Philippine Government.[62]

Thirdly, the ICJ stated that immunity before the courts of other states would cease once the person ceases to hold the office of Minister of Foreign Affairs. A court of one state may try a former foreign minister of another state in respect of acts committed before or after his period of office, or acts committed during that

---

60 *R. v. Bow Street Metropolitan Stipendiary Magistrate, ex parte Pinochet Ugarte (No. 3)* [2000] 1 AC 147 at 199 *per* Lord Browne-Wilkinson.

61 *In Re Grand Jury Proceedings, John Doe, No. 700*, 817 F 2d 1108 (United States Court of Appeals of the 4th Circuit, 1987).

62 See also *In Re Estate of Marcos Human Rights Litigation: Trajano v. Marcos*, 978 F 2d 493 (United States Court of Appeals for the 9th Circuit, 1992); *Hilao v. Estate of Marcos*, 103 F 3d 767 at 776–8 (United States Court of Appeals for the 9th Circuit, 1996); and *Estate of Domingo v. Republic of Philippines*, 808 F 2d 1349 (United States Court of Appeals for the 9th Circuit, 1987).

office 'in a private capacity'.[63] The Court provided no assistance as to what would or would not be a private act. And it did not indicate whether it agreed with Lord Browne-Wilkinson in *Pinochet No. 3* that acts such as torture or disappearance or genocide could never be committed in an official capacity and therefore fell to be treated as private acts. As noted above, Lord Browne-Wilkinson had said in *Pinochet No. 3* case:

> Can it be said that the commission of a crime which is an international crime against humanity and *jus cogens* is an act done in an official capacity on behalf of the state? I believe there to be strong ground for saying that the implementation of torture as defined by the Torture Convention cannot be a state function.[64]

Moreover, in the case of Mr Yerodia, he ceased to be Foreign Minister in November 2000, when he became Education Minister, and ceased to be a minister at all in April 2001. By the time the Court heard the case, and certainly when it gave its judgment, he was a former Foreign Minister.

Fourthly, and most significantly for present purposes, the ICJ said that its judgment would not preclude the ICC from exercising jurisdiction, since the ICC Statute

---

[63] *Congo* v. *Belgium*, note 8 above, para. 61.

[64] *R.* v. *Bow Street Metropolitan Stipendiary Magistrate, ex parte Pinochet Ugarte (No. 3)* [2000] 1 AC 147 at 203.

expressly precluded claims of immunity by any person, including serving foreign ministers or prime ministers or presidents. Thus, when it comes to serving foreign ministers, the principle of complementarity is trumped, and only the ICC (or other international criminal tribunals with jurisdiction) may claim and exercise jurisdiction.

The ICJ's judgment leaves unanswered a number of important questions. Can torture or genocide ever be authorised by a foreign minister as an official act? Do the functions of other persons – for example a serving deputy foreign minister, or a minister of education, or the special envoy of a president – mean that they too are entitled to immunity under customary international law? Does the grant of jurisdiction in an international convention imply absence of immunity in respect of a former head of state, as some of the majority in the House of Lords in *Pinochet* found? It is to be noted that, in its judgment in *Congo* v. *Belgium*, the ICJ stated that the mere fact that various international conventions imposed obligations of prosecution or extradition was not of itself sufficient to reach a conclusion that those conventions removed any entitlement to immunity. As the Court put it: 'jurisdiction does not imply absence of immunity.'[65]

---

65 *Congo* v. *Belgium*, note 8 above, para. 59.

Conclusions

The *Pinochet* and *Yerodia* cases were different – the distinction between a former president or minister and a serving president or minister is an important one. But the underlying issues are essentially the same. The judgments of the House of Lords (a national court) in *Pinochet* and of the ICJ in *Yerodia* reflect, in my opinion, a struggle between two competing visions of international law. For the majority in the House of Lords, international law is treated as a set of rules the primary purpose of which is to give effect to a set of broadly shared values, including a commitment to rooting out impunity for the gravest international crimes. The other vision, that reflected in the judgment of the ICJ, sees the rules of international law as being intended principally to facilitate relations between states, which remain the principal international actors. For the majority in the House of Lords, the balance is to be achieved by limiting the role of immunities and establishing, in effect, a presumption against immunity.

For the ICJ, on the other hand, there is a presumption in favour of immunity – including before national courts – unless it has been removed by express act. The ICJ's response to the Congo claim, and indirectly to the *Pinochet* decision, suggests a more limited role for national courts, certainly insofar as higher officials (presidents, foreign ministers etc.) are concerned, while they are in office and possibly even after they have left office, depending on how the notion of 'private acts' is interpreted and applied. In effect what the ICJ seems to be saying is that the little fish can be fried in the local courts, but for the more senior officials – or the decision-makers – only the international courts will do.

Should we care about which view prevails? Will it make a practical difference for the future shape of the emerging international criminal justice system? In asking those questions I am reminded of a visit which I made to Vukovar and its surrounding villages in the autumn of 2000. You will recall that Vukovar is the city that was the subject of a mass atrocity in November 1991, when Serb forces entered the main hospital at Vukovar, removed the non-Serbs, transported them several kilometres away to a place called Ovcara, and there killed more than 200 persons. That place is less than two hours' flying time from London. The person under whose command those killings are alleged to have taken place is called Colonel Mile Mrksic, and for those acts he has been indicted since 1995 by the ICTY for grave breaches of the Geneva Conventions of 1949, for violations of the laws of war, and for crime against humanity.[66] The same acts are the subject of a genocide case brought by Croatia at the ICJ against Yugoslavia (Serbia and Montenegro).[67]

During our visit to a small village outside Vukovar we were introduced to a very elderly lady who took us to what remained of her home. She took us to the cellar, and described through a translator how grenades had been lobbed into the basement, killing her husband and maiming her daughter. She remained in the cellar for two days, too frightened to come out. We asked if she knew who had carried out the acts. She looked surprised, then said 'Of course'. We asked who they were. She responded that it was neighbours from the next village, whom she saw once a week when she went shopping in the communal shop. We asked why they hadn't been arrested or prosecuted. She said because of a 'deal'. In this way we learnt of an understanding which had been reached between the UN/EU and departing Serbian forces, apparently to the effect that only a limited number of persons suspected of international

---

[66] *Prosecutor* v. *Mrksic, Radic, Sljivaucanin and Dokmanovic,* ICTY, Case No. IT-95-13a (Initial Indictment, 7 November 1995), www.un.org/icty/indictment/english/mrk-ii951107e.htm.

[67] *Republic of Croatia* v. *Federal Republic of Yugoslavia, Case Concerning Application of the Convention on the Prevention and Punishment of the Crime of Genocide,* ICJ, General List Case No. 118.

crimes (we were told that the number was twenty-five) would be prosecuted before the local courts for atrocities committed in the period between 1991 and 1995. That was apparently the price that had to be paid to obtain the voluntary departure of Serb forces.

As a result, the vast majority of individuals responsible for international crimes in and around Vukovar will never be brought to justice, before the Croatian or Serbian courts, or before the national courts of any other states, or before the ICTY. Even though Croatia has ratified the Statute of the ICC, they cannot be brought before that Court because it will only have jurisdiction over crimes occurring after 1 July 2002. Is impunity a price worth paying?

That question can be addressed at a number of levels. Lawyers are particularly interested in the *minutiae* of technical questions. Is there universal jurisdiction? When can immunity from jurisdiction be claimed? And so on. But what matters to most people is a bigger question: is the emerging system of international criminal justice fulfilling its objectives? And that question requires us to focus on what the objectives are. One commentator has identified the principal justifications as including punishment and justice (the Nuremberg and Tokyo tribunals), retribution and deterrence (the Eichmann trial in the Israeli courts), historical educa-

tion (the Demjanjuk proceedings) and the maintenance of international peace and security (the former
Yugoslavia).[68] In the sentencing phase of the *Erdemovic*
case, the Trial Chamber of the ICTY observed that
'[d]iscovering the truth is a cornerstone of the rule of
law and a fundamental step on the way to reconciliation
... for it is truth ... that begins the healing process'.[69] So
the real question boils down to this: if we limit or
exclude the role of national courts – whether by enter-
ing into deals of the kind that may have been done at
Vukovar in 1998 or by applying rules which entitle
certain persons to immunities from the jurisdiction of
national courts – do we undermine the system of international justice? Do we make it more difficult to do
justice, to provide retribution, to deter, to educate, to
deliver international peace and security, to bring reconciliation, to heal?

That is not a question that lends itself to a straight
answer. Experience over the last fifty years – since

---

68 G. Simpson, 'War Crimes: A Critical Introduction', in T. L. H.
    McCormack and G. J. Simpson (eds.), *The Law of War Crimes:
    National and International Approaches* (Kluwer Law
    International, London and The Hague, 1997), p. 1 at p. 28.

69 *Prosecutor* v. *Drazen Erdemovic*, Case No. IT-96-22, Sentencing
    Judgment, 5 March 1998, Trial Chamber II, para. 21; cited in
    Kirsten Campbell, 'The Trauma of Justice' (2002), *Journal of
    Human Rights* (forthcoming), n. 46 and the accompanying text.

Nuremberg – indicates that international law and the system of international justice, such as it is, is about balance.

The ICJ's approach will be embraced by those calling for limits on national prosecutions – such as Henry Kissinger in his recent book[70] – on the grounds that they interfere with the conduct of foreign relations. The balance between sovereign respect and the conduct of foreign relations, on the one hand, and the prosecution of criminal justice, on the other, will always be a difficult one to reach. But broad presumptions in favour of immunities – as reflected in the ICJ's recent decision – can only lead to a diminished role for national courts, a watered-down system of international criminal justice, and greater impunity.

[70] Henry Kissinger, *Does America Need a Foreign Policy?: Toward a Diplomacy for the 21st Century* (Simon & Schuster, New York and London, 2001).

4

The drafting of the Rome Statute

JAMES CRAWFORD

Introduction

The International Criminal Court (ICC) may or may
not be ultimately judged a success. But the Rome
Statute of 17 July 1998, establishing the Court, is already
a success in two ways. First, it has come into force with
substantial backing from many countries and despite
the unhappy and extravagant opposition of the United
States. Secondly, it is a significant step away from the
culture of impunity which until the 1990s accompanied
the elaboration of many international criminal law
instruments. Such success has many parents, and there
will be many to claim parentage of the Rome Statute for
an International Criminal Court, to claim responsibility for its conception, for its drafting, for this or that
provision.

In my own case I had nothing to do with the diplomatic
process of drafting the Statute in the period from 1995.
My role was more removed. To put it metaphorically,

I had something to do with the grandparent of the Rome Statute – the Draft Statute of 1994 produced by the United Nations International Law Commission (ILC). In 1994, I chaired the ILC working group that produced the Draft Statute.[1] That Draft Statute got the diplomatic ball rolling again, after it had stopped in the early 1950s at the outset of the Cold War. It formed the initial text for consideration by the Preparatory Commission. It is true that the Draft Statute of 1994 was no more than a point of

[1]   Generally on the Rome Statute, see W. A. Schabas, *Introduction to the International Criminal Court* (Cambridge University Press, Cambridge, 2001); A. Cassese, P. Gaeta and J. R. W. D. Jones (eds.), *The Rome Statute of the International Criminal Court: A Commentary* (Oxford University Press, Oxford, 2002). See also M. C. Bassiouni, *The Statute of the International Criminal Court: A Documentary History* (Transnational Publishers, Ardsley, NY, 1998); R. S. Lee (ed.), *The International Criminal Court: The Making of the Rome Statute: Issues, Negotiations, Results* (Kluwer Law International, The Hague, 1999); M. Politi and G. Nesi (eds.), *Rome Statute of the International Criminal Court: A Challenge to Impunity* (Ashgate, Aldershot, 2001); L. N. Sadat, *The International Criminal Court and the Transformation of International Law: Justice for the New Millennium* (Transnational Publishers, Ardsley, NY, 2002); D. Shelton (ed.), *International Crimes, Peace and Human Rights: The Role of the International Criminal Court* (Transnational Publishers, Ardsley, NY, 2000); O. Triffterer (ed.), *Commentary on the Rome Statute of the International Criminal Court: Observers' Notes, Article by Article* (Nomos Verlag, Baden-Baden, 1999); H. A. M. von Hebel, J. G. Lammers and J. Schukking, *Reflections on the International Criminal Court: Essays in Honour of Adriaan Bos* (T. M. C. Asser Press, The Hague, 1999).

departure. There were to be many departures, conceptually and on points of detail. The individual which has emerged is, we might say, more robust and much more ambitious than its grandparent. But the affiliation is certain enough, and the differences between the generations are worth analysis.

This is not the place to go into detailed issues of the drafting of the Statute from a technical point of view. Rather, I want to look at the underlying issues which arose during the process of elaborating the Statute. Formally, that process stretched from 1993 up to 1998. Indeed, it has continued after the adoption of the Statute, which – continuing the analogy – may be said to have been delivered before term. Subsequent drafting exercises have included Rules of Procedure and Evidence and in particular the Elements of Crimes, which elaborates at length upon the crimes within the jurisdiction of the Court in order to provide authoritative guidance to the judges in its interpretation.[2] Moreover, that process is not yet finished. It is envisaged

2 Report of the Preparatory Commission for the International Criminal Court, 2 November 2000, UN Doc. PCNICC/2000/1; Rules of Procedure and Evidence, UN Doc. PCNICC/2000/1/Add.1; Elements of Crimes, UN Doc. PCNICC/2000/1/Add.2. See generally R. S. Lee (ed.), *The International Criminal Court: Elements of Crimes and Rules of Procedure and Evidence* (Transnational Publishers, Ardsley, NY, 2000).

that, in due course, there will be a further document elaborating on the crime of aggression, which crime will be inoperative as part of the Statute until that happens (if it ever does).

In a deeper sense, the process of elaboration started with the General Assembly resolution of 1946 endorsing the Nuremberg Charter, which envisaged that some more permanent arrangement would be made. It continued with the Genocide Convention of 1948, which specifically envisaged that an international criminal court would be established to try persons suspected of genocide. It then went underground for a prolonged period, only to come back to life after the end of the Cold War, in a very different legal and political environment but with essentially the same underlying issues unresolved and now back once more on the agenda.

Three underlying issues

What were those issues? I would identify three of them: an institutional problem (how to create a real international criminal court, with all that that implies), a legitimacy problem (how to validate that institution against international law's own demands for the rights of someone accused of a serious crime) and a political problem (how to make such a real international court acceptable to states in general). Before discussing the solutions adopted, I should say something about these three problems, putting each in historical perspective.

The institutional problem

The first problem was how to bridge the enormous gap, amounting to a chasm, between national and international institutions and processes in the field of criminal law. The ICC as a new institution had to be able to cope, potentially at once, with all the practical problems of successful investigation, prosecution, trial and punishment of very serious crimes. National criminal justice systems have evolved over many years and have the advantage of a territorial base, a police force, prosecution services with executive power, gaols, etc. By contrast, the ICC would be a territorially disembodied criminal court lacking independent executive powers. In terms of experience, it would be, metaphorically, a child. But this child would – having regard to the seriousness of the crimes and their consequences – have to be immediately capable of acting as an adult.

This recalls a passage from one of Montesquieu's *Persian Letters*, letter 94, entitled 'International law and its distortions'. The letter purports to be dated 1716; the collection of letters first appeared in 1721. Here Montesquieu is setting up an ideal of international law as a set of universal values, against a branch of law which 'explains to kings how far they can violate justice without damaging their own interests'. The allegedly Persian writer of the letter criticises this latter version of the subject, the Hobbesian version of *raison d'état*. Drawing on an equally venerable tradition, he writes to his friend:

> You would almost think ... that there were two entirely different types of justice: one, regulating the affairs of private individuals, rules civil law; the other, regulating the differences that arise between nations, tyrannizes over international law; as if international law were not itself a kind of civil law, not indeed the law of a particular country, but of the world.[3]

In this universalist tradition, international law is seen as 'a kind of civil law', a civil law of the world. But even the letter writer did not believe this literally: like Grotius, he did not conceive of international institutions. 'As between citizens, judges have to administer justice; as between nations, each nation has to adminis-

3   Montesquieu, *Persian Letters* (Penguin, revised edn, 1993), p. 176.

ter it itself.'[4] Civil law there may have been, but there was no civil process, still less any criminal process. According to that tradition, it might be possible, eventually, to establish inter-state arbitral tribunals. In effect these were surrogate decision-makers for states who could not or would not agree. But civil or criminal justice was the prerogative of states.

Now it is often said or assumed that we are past all this, that international law has moved from being an inter-state law to being something more. Substantively that is no doubt true, at least to some degree. But looking at the question from the point of view of institutions or processes, the position is much more difficult. Indeed, some would say the chasm still exists: 'you can't get there from here', as the *Punch* cartoon has the country yokel telling the city motorist who stops to ask the way to some destination.

But again, the optimist says, things have changed: something that can be described as a real international process has developed, not just an inter-state law about people, but a law applicable for and to people. It is relevant to recall the famous declaration of the Nuremberg Tribunal:

---

4   *Ibid.* (Letter 95).

> Crimes against international law are committed by
> men, not by abstract entities, and only by punishing
> individuals who commit such crimes can the
> provisions of international law be enforced.[5]

There was some element of circularity in the word 'only', since international law is enforced and applied daily against abstract entities. But of course it is not enforced by criminal process. The idea that states as such can be subject to criminal process or punishment has gained very little acceptance, and it was deliberately rejected by the ILC in its Articles on Responsibility of States for Internationally Wrongful Acts (2001). What the Nuremberg Tribunal seems to have been saying is that the only way of enforcing international criminal law is by punishing the individuals who commit those crimes. But the question it faced was whether there *was* any international criminal law, properly so-called, and that question was not answered by declaring that international criminal law can only be enforced against individuals.

When the optimist is pressed to justify this optimism about the existence of a real international process capable of bridging the chasm between the inter-state and the human dimensions, two examples are usually given.

[5]   International Military Tribunal (Nuremberg), Judgment and Sentences, (1947) 41 *American Journal of International Law* 172 at 221.

The first is the post-Nuremberg development of international criminal law. The second is the development not merely of human rights standards but of international courts and committees before which individuals have standing to invoke international law.

These are no doubt striking developments, but how far they go in the direction of a real international process is less clear. One might argue that they make it more difficult. The first development has, paradoxically, made it more difficult to solve the institutional problem. The second difficulty has, paradoxically, made it more difficult to solve the rule of law problem.

As to international criminal law, when the Nuremberg Charter was adopted in 1945, there was little by way of a set of international criminal laws appropriate for application by an international war crimes tribunal. Moreover, the crimes in the Nuremberg Charter – waging aggressive war, war crimes and associated crimes against humanity – were applicable only to selected defeated belligerents in the war. The charges of victor's justice and retrospective law were made at the time, and were a source of unease. Attempts were accordingly made to institute and generalise the outcome of Nuremberg, and three things were done in the period to 1950 to achieve that. First, the General Assembly in a non-binding resolution endorsed the Nuremberg Charter and expressed the view that the substantive crimes embodied in the Charter reflected customary international law.[6] Secondly, the Genocide Convention of 1948 elaborated the first and worst of the crimes against humanity as a specific crime.[7] Thirdly, the 1949 Geneva Conventions provided a reasonably comprehensive set of rules for the conduct of international armed conflict, grave breaches of which were to be punishable by states parties before their own courts or military tribunals. The 1949 Conventions also provided embryonically for standards of conduct in internal armed conflict, although they made provision for implementation or punishment.[8]

6   See the Charter of the International Military Tribunal, (1945) 39 *American Journal of International Law*, Supplement of Official Documents, p. 258; endorsed by the UN General Assembly in General Assembly Resolution 95 (I) of 11 December 1946.

7   Convention on the Prevention and Punishment of the Crime of Genocide, 9 December 1948, General Assembly Resolution 260 (III) A, 78 UNTS 277.

8   Geneva Convention for the Amelioration of the Condition of the Wounded and Sick in Armed Forces in the Field, 12 August 1949, 75 UNTS 31; Geneva Convention for the Amelioration of the Condition of Wounded, Sick and Shipwrecked Members of Armed Forces at Sea, 12 August 1949, 75 UNTS 85; Geneva Convention Relative to the Treatment of Prisoners of War, 12 August 1949, 75 UNTS 135; and Geneva Convention Relative to the Protection of Civilian Persons in Time of War, 12 August 1949, 75 UNTS 287.

In the early 1950s, work was underway on two further steps towards an international criminal jurisdiction – a study by the ILC on the possibility of an international criminal court, and a General Assembly working group on the definition of aggression. This was the situation when the curtain of the Cold War came down, and these new steps were frustrated. The ILC reported on the possibility of an international criminal court, and its report was shelved.[9] The General Assembly subcommittee laboured for years on the definition of aggression, producing eventually, in 1974, a text of such vagueness and imprecision as to be incapable of practical application in any difficult case.[10] There the issue of an international criminal court remained.

Instead, international criminal law developments flowed into new channels. Starting with the Single Convention on Narcotic Drugs,[11] a long line of treaties dealt with the suppression of crimes of international

---

[9] Report of the International Law Commission on the Question of International Criminal Jurisdiction, UN Doc. A/CN.4/15 (1950), reprinted in *Yearbook of the International Law Commission 1950*, vol. II, p. 1.

[10] General Assembly Resolution 3314 (XXIX), Definition of Aggression, 14 December 1974.

[11] Single Convention on Narcotic Drugs, New York, 30 March 1961, 520 UNTS 151; reprinted as amended by the Protocol Amending the Single Convention on Narcotic Drugs, New York, 8 August 1975, 976 UNTS 105.

concern. They covered drug trafficking, aircraft hijacking and other crimes against civil aviation, ship hijacking, a range of specifically defined terrorist crimes, and a number of other miscellaneous matters such as state torture and the employment of mercenaries. These suppression treaties did not seek to be comprehensive. They dealt with different questions, one after another. But there were many of them, and over time they came to cover much of the field of crimes of international concern. When events occurred which showed that there were gaps in coverage, they might be filled, as with the convention on ship hijacking of 1988, which followed the *Achille Lauro* affair.[12] In a number of areas there were supplementary conventions which were more comprehensive and ambitious in their coverage, in particular drug trafficking and, more recently, terrorism. (It has still not proved possible to produce a comprehensive definition of terrorism, but the patchwork definition of terrorism provided by the existing conventions has served almost the same function. It does not, however, cover crashing jet planes into skyscrapers, unless one classifies the planes as bombs.)

[12] Convention on the Suppression of Unlawful Acts Against the Safety of Maritime Navigation, Rome, 10 March 1988, 1678 UNTS 221. See also A. Cassese, *Terrorism, Politics and Law: The Achille Lauro Affair* (Polity Press, Cambridge, 1989).

On the whole, these developments took us further away from, not closer to, an international criminal court. Indeed, it is not too much to say that the development of international criminal law from the 1950s until the early 1990s was a development away from international to national jurisdiction. The original idea of generalising Nuremberg faded quickly. Before 1998, there were only two references in treaties to an international criminal court to be established – in Article VI of the Genocide Convention of 1948, repeated in Article V of the much less accepted Apartheid Convention of 1973. Instead of international jurisdiction, the suppression treaties worked on the basis of national courts exercising extended (but not universal[13]) jurisdiction, and they applied without prejudice to the concurrent or more extensive jurisdiction of national courts over locally defined crimes. In terms of international process, the suppression treaties focused on inter-state co-operation and extended national jurisdiction. Thus the international instruments effectively provided for the extension of national process and jurisdiction. There was no international criminal process as such. When the international criminal court idea took off

---

[13] As noted by President Guillaume in the *Arrest Warrant Case (Democratic Republic of the Congo v. Belgium)*, Judgment of 14 February 2002, Separate Opinion, especially para. 16.

again in the 1990s, it was against the trend of development of the previous forty years.[14]

Moreover, because these international treaties
focused on national courts and conferred supplementary, non-exclusive jurisdiction, they did not need to
focus very clearly on any threshold for jurisdiction in
terms of the gravity or systematic character of the
crimes covered. Individual acts covered by the suppression treaties could be relatively routine or minor (e.g.
most forms of retail drug trafficking), or at least they
could be not very different in quality from serious
national crimes (e.g. local acts of terrorism).
Jurisdiction over them might be extended, but the acts
themselves, considered in isolation, were nothing out of
the ordinary. By contrast, an international criminal
court could not possibly be given jurisdiction over run-
of-the-mill drug trafficking cases or it would risk being
swamped. Clearly, a high threshold for ICC jurisdiction
was required – yet that threshold was not articulated in
the suppression treaties, which made up the bulk of
international criminal law.

It is true that there had been a few developments at the
upper end of the scale of international gravity, to go
alongside the Genocide Convention and the four

[14] See generally D. McClean, *International Co-operation in Civil
and Criminal Matters* (Oxford University Press, Oxford, 2002).

Geneva Conventions of 1949. But these made only limited progress. The two 1977 Protocols to the Geneva Conventions developed the range of prohibitions in the field of international and to a lesser extent internal armed conflict, but did not add any new institutional elements of any significance.[15] The 1973 Convention on the Suppression and Punishment of the Crime of Apartheid treated apartheid as a separate and special phenomenon, confined essentially to southern Africa.[16] This was politically understandable at the time, but it tended to separate the crime of apartheid from its proper conceptual basis as a crime against humanity – that is to say, as a *systematic* crime involving large-scale, violent or coercive oppression of one human group by another.

Moreover, there were serious gaps. The attempt to define aggression had run into the sands. The scope of the international law concerning the conduct of internal armed conflict was still rudimentary, contested and lacking any form of enforcement provision. There was

[15] Protocol Additional to the Geneva Conventions of 12 August 1949, and Relating to the Protection of Victims of International Armed Conflicts (Protocol I), Geneva, 8 June 1977, 1125 UNTS 3; Protocol Additional to the Geneva Conventions of 12 August 1949, and Relating to the Protection of Victims of Non-International Armed Conflicts (Protocol II), Geneva, 8 June 1977, 1125 UNTS 609.

[16] International Convention on the Suppression and Punishment of the Crime of Apartheid, 30 November 1973, 1015 UNTS 243.

no agreed international definition of crimes against humanity, still less a convention dealing with that subject. Yet (with the possible exception of terrorism, which itself had escaped comprehensive definition) the two most common and most serious problems, at the high end of the spectrum of international crimes, were crimes against humanity and war crimes in internal armed conflict. Moreover, while the suppression conventions had been quite widely used as part of the fight against transboundary crime, the enforcement of the international law prohibitions against genocide and international war crimes was minimal. Only in a handful of cases (Eichmann, Calley) were these rules enforced at all. Large-scale crimes in Cambodia and elsewhere (crimes against humanity at least, possibly genocide) had gone entirely unaddressed.

To summarise, the institutional problem in the early 1990s was huge. There had been no experience of the international administration of criminal justice since the 1940s. Attempts to establish an international criminal court had run into the sands and were widely seen as utopian. International criminal law had developed in a different direction, and the enforcement of crimes which were inherently international in character or context (genocide, war crimes) had been almost entirely ineffective.

The rule of law problem

Then there is a second, related problem. An international criminal court would have to be seen as legitimate, to comply with standards for the rule of law which we have come to expect from national criminal justice systems. Yet it would (probably) only operate on an occasional basis. This created an issue for international human rights and the rule of law. It was of particular importance in criminal cases. The major international human rights treaties – the International Covenant of 1966, the European Convention on Human Rights and Fundamental Freedoms, etc. – give ten times as much attention to criminal as to civil justice. Surely an international criminal tribunal must comply with international law's own standards for criminal law in general? For example, could it be an occasional institution which was at the same time 'established by law'?

This was not the lesson international criminal lawyers drew from international human rights instruments. At least there were international human rights courts and committees where the individual had standing – the European Court of Human Rights, for example. Here, it was said, was a process of sorts, involving both the state and individuals as parties asserting their own rights. But the analogy is misleading. International human rights processes pit the individual against the state (not *vice versa*), and human rights operate – as they operate to a large extent even under the UK Human Rights Act 1998 – as a critical standard for the assessment of and eventually for remedying deficiencies in national law. They are not first order rules of conduct, in the way that criminal law rules are.

This is not to decry human rights law, which has been incrementally a huge force for change in the modern period. But international human rights courts still do not involve the civil process envisaged by Montesquieu, still less any criminal process. In practice, there has been no international process by which states could call individuals to account, and this omission was deliberate.[17] There can, for example, be no counterclaims for breach of international standards brought against individual claimants, whether before human rights tribunals or (it seems) in direct recourse arbitration under bilateral investment treaties.[18] These fora are essentially unilateral, against the state which

[17] For the application of human rights standards to non-state entities, see generally A. Clapham, *Human Rights in the Private
Sphere* (Clarendon Press, Oxford, 1993).

[18] As to which see J. Paulsson, 'Arbitration Without Privity' (1995)
10 *ICSID Review-FILJ* 232.

has joined in establishing them and which has consented to be sued. By confining the individual to the role of claimant the problem of due process is side-stepped. The individual consents to the system in the very act of invoking it. But no one consents to be a criminal accused.

The existence of international human rights courts, especially the European Court of Human Rights, may have had some value in showing the possibility of standing mixed tribunals at the international level. But they were a far cry from an international criminal court. And, in the field of criminal law, the critical standard, as it has developed in the human rights jurisprudence, makes it difficult indeed for an international tribunal. In particular, criminal courts must be 'established by law' and must follow the rule of law. How could an international criminal court be 'established by law' when it would lack many features of national criminal justice systems? For example, its power to compel evidence would be limited. In terms of its functioning it was likely to be an occasional court. Only a few of the possible cases would be likely to come before it, yet the basis for selecting these was unclear and might well be arbitrary. Even venerable national institutions – for example, the *conseils d'état* of Luxembourg and other countries – have been held not to be established by law but to need significant reform.[19]

So to the age-old structural problem was added a rule of law problem: were we to establish international criminal processes that did not meet international law's standards for criminal processes anywhere? That would be a curious form of universalism. Or, in moving to an international criminal process, were we to make an exception, to fall below our own standards? It may seem that we are unable to get there from here. As Churchill is reputed to have said, it is unsafe and unsatisfactory to leap a chasm in two bounds. And yet it might seem impossible to leap it in one.

It is true that there are occasions which cry out for some form of international trial process. But when we establish international criminal courts we are haunted by the rule of law problem, as Nuremberg and Tokyo were haunted. Are these courts established by law? Is this victor's justice? Is this criminal law in truth retrospective, since international law has never been accompanied by international criminal process and we have instead relied on national law to legitimise trials? It has not taken much

[19] See *Procola* v. *Luxembourg*, Judgment, 28 September 1995, ECHR, Application No. 14570/89; and *McGonnell* v. *United Kingdom*, Judgment, 8 February 2000, ECHR, Application No. 28488/95.

imagination for Mr Milosevic's counsellors to think of these points. They have been often made before, in Judge Pal's dissent at Tokyo, for example, and in the conscientious concerns of other lawyers who nonetheless voted 'yes' to convictions at those trials.[20]

After 1989, the same old issues emerged out of cold war storage, you might say. The Yugoslavia and Rwanda Tribunals were the Nuremberg and Tokyo Tribunals of our time, and they raised exactly similar concerns, but now they did so against the very human rights standards which had been perhaps the greatest international achievement of the preceding forty years.

How did the new *ad hoc* tribunals respond when their legitimacy was queried against these standards? Essentially in two ways: on the military tribunal analogy; and on the basis that the international arena is special, and is not subject to international standards applicable to national courts. The challenge was raised before the ICTY Appeals Chamber in an early case, *Prosecutor* v. *Tadic*.[21] It was argued that, because the

---

[20] See R. N. Sanyal (ed.), *International Military Tribunal for the Far East: Dissentient Judgment of Justice Pal* (Sanyal & Co., Calcutta, 1953), pp. 697–701. See also B. V. A. Röling and A. Cassese, *The Tokyo Trial and Beyond: Reflections of a Peacemonger* (Polity Press, Cambridge, 1993).

[21] *Prosecutor* v. *Tadic* (Jurisdiction), Appeals Chamber, 2 October 1995, 106 ILR 453.

ICTY was established as an occasional *ad hoc* body by a Security Council resolution, it was not established by law as required by the International Covenant or the European Convention on Human Rights. The Appeals Chamber responded as follows:

> [The] appellant has not satisfied this Chamber that the requirements laid down in these … conventions must apply not only in the context of national legal systems but also with respect to proceedings conducted before an international court. This Chamber is … satisfied that the principle that a tribunal must be established by law … is a general principle of law imposing an international obligation which only applies to the administration of criminal justice in a municipal setting. It follows from this principle that it is incumbent on all States to organise their system of criminal justice in such a way as to ensure that all individuals are guaranteed the right to have a criminal charge determined by a tribunal established by law. This does not entail, however, that, by contrast, an international criminal court could be set up at the mere whim of a group of governments. Such a court ought to be rooted in the rule of law and offer all guarantees embodied in the relevant international instruments. Then the court may be said to be 'established by law'.[22]

There are several problems with this. It seems wrong in principle to say that international criminal process is

[22] *Ibid.*, pp. 472–3.

subject to a lesser standard than national criminal process. This is certainly true when we conceive of the relevant values as human *rights*. How can my right to be tried by an impartial and independent tribunal established by law be abrogated because the tribunal is established at the international level? Are states free to violate international human rights when they hunt in packs – so to speak? It is true that there are institutional difficulties when conduct affecting individual rights is carried out not by states but by international organisations, that is, by associations of states. The European Court of Human Rights has no jurisdiction over the European Union or over NATO, and the conduct in question may be attributed to the collectivity, not to its members.[23] But it is one thing to admit to an institutional gap and another to say that the underlying standard is inapplicable in principle.[24] Anyway, there was no obvious institutional gap for

---

[23] *Bankovic* v. *Belgium and 16 Other Contracting States*, Decision on Admissibility, 12 December 2001, ECHR, Application No. 52207/99.

[24] See generally P. Klein, *La Responsabilité des Organisations Internationales dans les Ordres Juridiques Internes et en Droit des Gens* (Bruylant, Brussels, 1998); A. Reinisch, *International Organizations Before National Courts* (Cambridge University Press, Cambridge, 2000); P. Sands and P. Klein, *Bowett's Law of International Institutions* (Sweet & Maxwell, London, 2001); K. Wellens, *Remedies Against International Organisations* (Cambridge University Press, Cambridge, 2002).

the Appeals Chamber. The Chamber was authorised to apply international law and the ICTY as an international court could have refused to act, except as permitted by international law.

Furthermore, it is easy to see that the International Covenant does not equate the specific due process standards with the requirement that a criminal court be established by law. Those standards are separately expressed in the Covenant (and in the European Convention). Under the Covenant, everyone is entitled in the first place – over and above specific issues of due process and the right to defend oneself – to 'a competent, independent and impartial tribunal established by law'. A body whose existence was precarious or whose judges were selected arbitrarily might not meet this standard, even if the accused had a full right of legal representation and was not compelled to confess guilt.

To be fair, the Appeals Chamber went on to give reasons why it could be considered to be established by law, even in the context of a Security Council resolution, i.e. an executive resolution.[25] The Security Council did have power to establish the Tribunal in terms of the United Nations Charter. The Tribunal's mandate had been affirmed and substantial resources for its work

[25] *Prosecutor* v. *Tadic* (Jurisdiction), Appeals Chamber, 2 October 1995, 105 ILR 453 at 465–71 and 474.

provided by the General Assembly; support for the Tribunal was, if not quite universal, widespread. The Tribunal was not established only on a temporary basis but had a long-term mandate in terms of charges of war crimes in Yugoslavia. Moreover, the support for it was manifested by national legislation in many countries, providing for co-operation and supporting the process of the Court with ancillary national processes. All of this gave it the combined legitimacy which was associated with the rule of law, even if it had its origin in a collective executive resolution of an emergency character.

Thus we can accept the conclusion of the Appeals Chamber in the *Tadic* case, if not all of its reasoning. But it showed that there was a difficulty in creating an international criminal court, to ensure that international law's standards were fully met.

The problem of acceptability of a universal international criminal court

Above all, perhaps, there was the problem of the acceptability of an international criminal court for states. How would it relate to national criminal courts with their own jurisdiction over the alleged crimes and the accused persons? No one defends genocide or the massacre of civilians in armed conflict. But armed conflict always produces what NATO spokesmen call 'collateral casualties'. If drawing the line between legitimate and illegitimate behaviour in wars – international or internal – was to be practically a justiciable matter, a matter for criminal courts on a regular basis, then the relation between national and international jurisdiction would become a very sharp question indeed. *Ad hoc* criminal courts were one thing – whether they were called into being to deal with Nazi or Japanese war criminals or with generals and militias in the former Yugoslavia and *genocidaires* in Rwanda. Such *ad hoc* creations were *a priori* controlled, more or less. They amounted to international criminal justice for others, from their inception. But the ICC was – potentially at least – international criminal justice for ourselves, not just for others. How could it be controlled?

This was a particular issue for international peacekeeping operations. Cases had occurred where those operations were alleged to have involved war crimes; there were investigations and even trials in Canada and Belgium.[26] Allegations were made that Western bomb-

26 Crimes committed by military personnel during United Nations peacekeeping operations in Somalia have been dealt with by military court martial in Canada: *R. v. Brocklebank*, Court Martial Appeal Court of Canada (1996) 134 DLR (4th) 377. Italy and Belgium also instituted inquiries into the conduct of their military personnel in Somalia: see e.g. the decision of

ing and targeting in Yugoslavia and subsequently Afghanistan involved breaches of international humanitarian law. So these were not just theoretical questions.

Two possible solutions

Faced with these three difficulties in the way of establishing an international criminal court, it was possible to envisage two broad solutions. One was essentially a procedural solution. The ICC would in effect borrow its legitimacy from a national system or systems of international criminal justice, acting as surrogate for these, exercising their jurisdiction and applying their substantive

the Belgian Military Court of 17 December 1997 in *Ministère public et Centre pour l'égalité des chances et la lutte contre le racisme* v. *C ... et B ...*, *Journal des Tribunaux*, 4 April 1998, p. 286. See also N. Lupi, 'Report by the Enquiry Commission on the Behaviour of Italian Peacekeeping Troops in Somalia' (1998) 1 *Yearbook of International Humanitarian Law* 375; R. M. Young and M. Molina, 'IHL and Peace Operations: Sharing Canada's Lessons Learned from Somalia' (1998) 1 *Yearbook of International Humanitarian Law* 362; K. Boustany, 'Brocklebank: A Questionable Decision of the Court Martial Appeal Court of Canada' (1998) 1 *Yearbook of International Humanitarian Law* 371; R. C. R. Siekmann, 'The Fall of Srebrenica and the Attitude of Dutchbat from an International Legal Perspective' (1998) 1 *Yearbook of International Humanitarian Law* 301.

law to the extent that the limited rules of international criminal law did not cover some question. The second solution was to establish, from the beginning, an essentially autonomous international criminal justice system, with its own institutions and rules, essentially distinct from national systems and dependent on them only for co-operation and enforcement.

In terms of the difficulty outlined above, the procedural model was strongest in addressing the first and, especially, the third, and weakest in relation to the second. Conversely, the international criminal justice system model would address the first difficulty head on, and in doing so would meet the second. But the more autonomous and independent the system created, the more problems one could envisage in terms of its real acceptability, especially *vis-à-vis* non-parties. Either the new system would impose itself on third parties, as national criminal justice systems do (absent any questions of immunity such as those raised in the *Pinochet* case[27]). Or it would apply only to nationals of states

27 *Re Augusto Pinochet Ugarte*, UK High Court of Justice, Queen's Bench Division (Divisional Court), 28 October 1998, (1999) 38 ILM 70; *R. v. Bow Street Metropolitan Stipendiary Magistrate, ex parte Pinochet Ugarte (No. 1)*, England, House of Lords, 25 November 1998, [2000] 1 AC 61; *R. v. Bow Street Metropolitan Stipendiary Magistrate, ex parte Pinochet Ugarte (No. 3)*, England, House of Lords, 24 March 1999, [2000] 1 AC 147.

parties, making the ICC a sort of international criminal court for the virtuous.

In 1994, the ILC proposed a text essentially reflecting the procedural model, and its proposal became the basis for the subsequent negotiations. In the course of the negotiations, however, the model changed, and in the Rome Statute and associated documents what has emerged is, in essence, a separate international criminal justice system. The drafting of the Rome Statute is the history of the move from the first to the second model.

The ILC's procedural model

The ILC's approach was to create an international criminal court which would in essence do for states what they could have done for themselves, having jurisdiction over an accused in respect of some grave crime under international law. If a particular state party to the Geneva Conventions of 1949 or to some other international criminal law convention had both custody of and jurisdiction over the accused, that custodial state could transfer the accused to the ICC – and at the same time in effect transfer its jurisdiction over the accused. Only then would the ICC proceed independently, although probably with the assistance of the ceding state. Conceptually, the case would proceed on the basis of the relevant crime under international law, any associated rules of international law, and the national law of the state or states where the crime was committed. This meant it was not necessary for the Statute of the Court to set out in detail all the elements of the crimes within its jurisdiction. It was sufficient to identify those crimes and to leave it to substantive international law, in conjunction with applicable national law where international law was silent on some matter, to deal with the substance. The ICC in this conception was an essentially procedural or remedial device. It did not require the creation of a new international criminal justice system, with all that that entailed.[28]

Central to the ILC's text was the idea of complementarity, a term intended to express the relationship between the ICC and national courts. There was much talk at the time of 'subsidiarity', the concept used in association with the Maastricht Treaty of 1992 to express the relationship between EU law and national law.[29] It was

---

[28] The evolution of the ILC's model can be traced in its Annual Reports to the General Assembly from 1992 to 1994: Report of the International Law Commission on a Draft Code of Crimes Against the Peace and Security of Mankind, UN GAOR, 47th Sess., Supp. No. 10, UN Doc. A/47/10, pp. 9–33; 48th Sess., Supp. No. 10, UN Doc. A/48/10, pp. 21–42; 49th Sess., Supp. No. 10, UN Doc. A/49/10, pp. 23–194.

[29] Treaty on European Union, Maastricht, 7 February 1992, 1757 UNTS 3, Preamble. See also A. G. Toth, 'The Principle of

not appropriate to describe an international criminal court as 'subsidiary' to national courts, but its role was certainly intended to be secondary. Anyhow, the term 'subsidiarity' was already taken, so 'complementarity' was used. It was useful in explaining to governments the limited role the ICC was intended to have, and in that sense it addressed the third, political problem described already. But its main function was in relation to the first problem, the underlying institutional issue. The ICC was essentially a guarantor of state compliance with the obligation to investigate credible allegations of war crimes involving persons on its territory. Referred to as the *aut dedere aut judicare* principle, that obligation requires states either themselves to try, or to extradite to some other requesting state for trial, persons found to have a case to answer for the relevant international crime. The ICC became an alternative forum for transfer, but the assumption was that in most cases the custodial state would proceed to trial itself. Any party to the ICC Statute

Subsidiarity in the Maastricht Treaty' (1992) 29 *Common Market Law Review* 1079. The principle of complementarity was emphasised in the preamble to the ILC's Draft Statute for an International Criminal Court, UN GAOR 49th Sess., Supp. No. 10, UN Doc. A/49/10, pp. 43–160: '[The international criminal court] is intended to be complementary to national criminal justice systems in cases where such trial procedures may not be available or may be ineffective.'

could trigger the *aut dedere aut judicare* obligation by making a complaint, which the Prosecutor could then take up.

This approach allowed the ILC to provide that state consent was the underlying basis of jurisdiction. Since the point of the Statute was to get custodial states to comply with their own existing obligations under international criminal law treaties, and since they could do so without transferring the accused for trial at the international level, it was not necessary to compel them to do so. Their consent to an international trial (and also the consent of the state where the crime was committed, i.e. the territorial state) was required. This powerfully met the third difficulty I have identified. States could become parties to the Statute without any ultimate commitment to agreeing to an international trial. They could support the international system in a range of ways while preserving their own jurisdiction with respect to persons subject to it. Not for the first time in international law, the text aimed at universality rather than the adoption of a system of compulsory jurisdiction.

There were, however, two exceptions to this principle of consent. First, the Security Council acting under Chapter VII of the Charter could override any consent required and submit a case or class of cases falling within the Statute to the ICC.[30] Such a decision would of course be subject to the veto. It was an essential element in order to deter the creation of still more *ad hoc* tribunals for international crimes. In effect the 1994 Draft Statute institutionalised (and thus removed the need for) any further *ad hoc* criminal tribunals being created by the Security Council, thereby at the same time addressing the rule of law problem and attempting an end-run around Chapter VII as a constitutional basis for criminal jurisdiction. Under the proposed Statute, international criminal jurisdiction was not created by an emergency executive resolution; it existed already, and was given effect by the implementing laws of the state parties. But the exercise of jurisdiction was triggered by the Security Council – an appropriate role in respect of situations covered by Chapter VII.

The second exception concerned the crime of genocide. The ILC's Draft Statute gave the proposed court 'automatic' jurisdiction over genocide, independently of the consent of the custodial or any other state.[31] This reflected the cardinal character of genocide as the 'worst of crimes'. From a technical point of view, it was justified by the fact that the Genocide Convention did not confer any form of extraterritorial jurisdiction over

[30] ILC's Draft Statute, Articles 23(1) and 25(4).
[31] *Ibid.*, Articles 20(a), 21(1)(a) and 25(1).

genocide, so that a state with custody of a person credibly accused of genocide in some other state apparently had no choice but to return the accused to the territorial state (which might be a step towards impunity) or to transfer him or her to the ICC. That choice was already reflected in Article VI of the Genocide Convention, as noted already. Thus the exception could be justified in terms of the existing law. But in substance it was a reflection of a view within the ILC that the complementarity approach was too pervasive and involved too many concessions to state sovereignty.

On the other hand, precisely because it relied on consent, complementarity and pre-existing international criminal law, the ILC's Draft Statute could accept a broader range of subject-matter jurisdiction. There was no need to limit the ICC to the Nuremberg crimes of aggression, war crimes and crimes against humanity (including genocide) – two of which were anyway undefined or only partially defined in international instruments. Experience – for example, with the Noriega affair and the Lockerbie bombing – showed that other crimes could have a pronounced international dimension and could be appropriate for an international criminal court. Thus the ILC's text extended jurisdiction over all the crimes defined by international treaties in force, and made provision for new treaty crimes to be added. It defined those crimes not autonomously but by reference to their definition in existing international law, thereby avoiding the need for an extensive new exercise in drafting. Instead of a jurisdictional bar (to avoid 'run-of-the-mill' treaty crimes coming before the ICC), there was an admissibility threshold, applied by the Prosecutor and reviewed by the Court and linked to the principle of complementarity.[32] Only cases of major significance, which could not be dealt with at the national level, would come to the ICC.

One of the major criticisms made of the ILC's model was that it gave no independent investigatory role to the Prosecutor, prior to the referral of a case and independently of the consent of the states concerned. Only once the pre-conditions for the exercise of jurisdiction were met could the Prosecutor act with full autonomy. This was certainly a deficiency; it was a concession to the

---

[32] *Ibid.*, Article 35. The principle of complementarity is also central to the determination of admissibility under Article 17 of the Rome Statute. See further, J. T. Holmes, 'The Principle of Complementarity', in R. S. Lee (ed.), *The International Criminal Court: The Making of the Rome Statute: Issues, Negotiations, Results* (Kluwer Law International, The Hague, 1999), p. 41; J. T. Holmes, 'Complementarity: National Courts Versus the ICC', in A. Cassese, P. Gaeta and J. R. W. D. Jones (eds.), *The Rome Statute of the International Criminal Court: A Commentary* (Oxford University Press, Oxford, 2002), p. 667.

concern expressed by some states that an independent Prosecutor with a roving commission to investigate international crimes would involve too great an infringement of sovereignty, even if the Prosecutor could not initiate a trial at the international level without the relevant consents. But it was an independent concession, which was not required by the complementarity model. The trigger for the *aut dedere aut judicare* obligation could just as well come from an international prosecutor as from a third state.

Overall, as this point showed, the ILC's Draft Statute of 1994 made major concessions to national jurisdiction in the interests of maximising support for the controversial idea of an ICC. Indeed, the principal point of the exercise was to get the idea of an ICC Statute to the stage of active discussion in a diplomatic forum. The kinds of objection to the ICC since made by the United States were not hard to predict; what was hard was to assess how the majority of states would respond to them. A very ambitious conception of an ICC might have joined the large pile of rejected proposals (going back to the 1930s). In case of doubt, therefore, the third problem, that of political acceptability, trumped the first and the second: it would be a matter for states to assess the possibility of further steps forward, assuming that the matter would be actively discussed at all.

The Rome Statute: an international criminal justice system for a few crimes?

I still believe that nothing more ambitious than the ILC's Draft Statute could have got on to the agenda in 1994, such was the combination of history, ennui and professional disbelief. Yet it is remarkable how rapidly the situation changed. A number of factors combined to produce the change. An obvious one was the enormous and increasing support given to the ICC idea by non-governmental organisations, which had previously been almost silent. A less obvious factor was the establishment of not one but two *ad hoc* tribunals under Chapter VII of the Charter. On the one hand, there were concerns as to the possible proliferation of criminal tribunals created *ad hoc*, and there was scepticism at the idea that a criminal tribunal could substitute for effective political and military measures to deal with a Chapter VII situation. On the other hand, the Security Council had shown that the apparently impossible was achievable. International criminal tribunals could be created and could function. A neglected factor was the increasing role of justice ministries in the negotiations. These delegates brought a range of professional concerns about the actual functioning of an ICC and its interaction with national legal and constitutional systems. To a certain extent, this cut across more traditional foreign affairs concerns as to loss of sovereignty and the paramountcy of inter-state relations.

Many of the provisions which emerged in the Rome Statute do not pertain to the choice between models of ICC jurisdiction, and do not need discussion here. For example, both the ILC's Draft Statute and the Rome Statute prohibit judges who have served a full term from being re-elected,[33] a provision which should probably be applied to all full-time international tribunals. Both texts provide for the ICC to consist of a mixture of judges with criminal trial experience and qualifications and those experienced in international criminal law and/or human rights.[34] In a number of respects the Rome Statute made independent improvements. There is now a more pronounced emphasis on gender equality[35] and on provisions for the compensation of victims;[36] in both respects, the Rome Statute is a clear advance on the ILC's Draft Statute.

For present purposes, however, I need to mention four issues which did pertain to the choice between models, and to compare the solutions proposed by the ILC with those finally adopted.

[33] ILC Draft Statute, Article 6(6); Rome Statute, Article 36(9).
[34] ILC Draft Statute, Article 6(1); Rome Statute, Article 36(3).
[35] Rome Statute, Article 36(8).   [36] *Ibid.*, Articles 75 and 79.

Consent, complementarity and the 'ownership' of crimes   From a fairly early stage in the negotiations in the Preparatory Commission, the idea of optional jurisdiction was virtually excluded. The majority agreed that states parties to the Statute should by virtue of their participation be treated as having accepted the jurisdiction of the Court. Under Article 12, the Court may exercise its jurisdiction provided that either the state of the accused's nationality or the state on whose territory the alleged crime was committed are parties to the Statute, or (if they are not parties) if either of them has accepted its jurisdiction *ad hoc*. By contrast, the custodial state has no specific role in determining jurisdiction.

Under this system, the requirement of separate consent to jurisdiction is removed for states parties to the Statute. Even with respect to states not parties, their lack of consent is irrelevant to jurisdiction, provided that either the state of the accused's nationality or the state on whose territory the crime was committed are parties. In this important sense the jurisdiction of the ICC is general and automatic.

As a corollary, the principle of complementarity has no effect in determining the existence of jurisdiction. To that extent it is reduced in significance, although it retains its force in terms of the *exercise* of jurisdiction. (The ILC's Draft Statute gave effect to it at both levels.)

As a further corollary, any state party to the Statute can refer a possible crime to the Prosecutor, irrespective of any lack of contact between the referring state and the crime.[37]

Thus no state party has a veto over prosecution, and the consent even of non-parties may be irrelevant with respect to crimes committed by their nationals abroad. To compensate for the reduction in the legal significance of the principle of complementarity at the level of jurisdiction, complementarity is given enhanced significance at the level of admissibility. The Preamble emphasises that 'the International Criminal Court under this Statute shall be complementary to national criminal jurisdictions'; complementarity is also mentioned in Article 1. The principle of complementarity is to be given effect by the Prosecutor in deciding whether to take forward an investigation, and by the Court in deciding whether to authorise a prosecution. A case is only admissible before the ICC where no state with jurisdiction over the crime is willing and able genuinely to carry forward the investigation (Article 17). On the other hand, it is a matter for the Court to determine admissibility; an investigating state can call upon it to do so but cannot predetermine the result (Article 18).

---

[37]   *Ibid.*, Article 14.

Thus states, whether parties or non-parties, may influence decisions on admissibility by diligently investigating such crimes themselves. But they do not have ultimate control over prosecution of their nationals for crimes committed abroad. On the other hand, except in cases where the nationals concerned are covered by some immunity (e.g. as diplomats or members of visiting armed forces), such ultimate control has never existed *vis-à-vis* national courts of third states. Moreover, while the Statute follows general international law in specifying that the official position of an accused, even as a head of state, is not a bar to the *exercise* of jurisdiction (Article 27), it also specifies that a request for surrender or co-operation may not be made if it would 'require the requested State to act inconsistently with its obligations under international law with respect to the State or diplomatic immunity of a person or property of a third State' (Article 98). Since there can be no trials *in absentia*, this makes it much less likely that serving officials of non-party states will come before the Court. But this is only legally excluded for those senior officials who stay at home.

The independent Prosecutor   Both the ILC's Draft Statute and the Rome Statute provided for an independent Prosecutor to conduct actual prosecutions. But the Rome Statute also gives the Prosecutor authority to investigate suspected crimes within the Court's jurisdiction without seeking any prior approval. 'The Prosecutor may initiate investigations *proprio motu* on the basis of information on crimes within the jurisdiction of the Court' (Article 15(1)). This is a major step forward, as already noted. But it is even more significant when it is combined with the abandonment of any stringent consent requirement on the part of states as a condition for the existence of jurisdiction. *Vis-à-vis* states parties to the Statute, as well as third states in certain cases, the Prosecutor will in principle be able to decide which crimes warrant preliminary investigation. Further and more detailed investigation requires the approval of a Pre-Trial Chamber, but again states, parties or non-parties, have no veto at this stage.

The scope of jurisdiction   In both these respects – the abolition of consent requirements and the independent powers of the Prosecutor – the Rome Statute is a significant step towards something which can be described as an international criminal justice system. On the other hand, there has been a significant reduction in the subject-matter of that system, i.e. in the crimes which fall within the Court's jurisdiction, particularly as compared with the ILC's proposals.

First, certain more or less temporary limitations should be noted.

Under Article 5(2), jurisdiction may not be exercised over the crime of aggression until the states parties have agreed on a definition of that crime and on modalities for the exercise of jurisdiction. The ILC had more simply proposed that no prosecution should be commenced for the crime of aggression unless the Security Council had first determined, in the exercise of its express power in Article 39 of the Charter, that the state concerned has committed aggression. The ILC's proposal was permanent in effect, whereas (unless it is adopted as a modality under Article 5(2)) the issue under the Rome Statute is likely to return to trouble the states parties.

In addition, Article 124 allows states parties to exclude war crimes committed on its territory or by its nationals from the Court's jurisdiction for a period of seven years. This bizarre exclusion of course had no parallel in the ILC's Draft Statute. It would appear to override the general requirements for jurisdiction under the Statute and to operate as a guarantee: in a case covered by a declaration under Article 124, the fact that some other state party concerned has not made such a declaration (e.g. the state where the crime was committed) would seem to be irrelevant.[38]

Of more long-term importance, and of more direct relevance to my theme, is the overall limitation of the Court's jurisdiction produced by Article 5. Jurisdiction is limited to four crimes: genocide, crimes against humanity, war crimes and (with the suspensive proviso noted already) the crime of aggression. It is a remarkable feature that the ICC's subject-matter jurisdiction began as a longish list of crimes defined by existing treaties in force, and ended as a detailed specification of a few crimes under international criminal law, without explicit reference to any existing treaties. The Rome Statute thus limits jurisdiction to only a few crimes, but redefines those crimes in detail. In effect, the Rome Statute is a new – but limited – code of international criminal law. It is true that, in many respects (especially in the case of genocide and international war crimes) its provisions follow, more or less verbatim, the language of the earlier conventions. On the other hand, they substantially develop the field of crimes in internal armed conflict, and, as to crimes against humanity, they constitute the very first authoritative treaty definition. Moreover, even in relation to the definitions which are

[38] It is an open question whether the same analysis applies to new parties acceding after the entry into force of the Statute (Article 11(2)).

transposed unchanged from earlier treaties, this is done without reference to whether the states parties to the Rome Statute are also parties to those treaties (for example, to the Genocide Convention or the 1977 Protocols), and without reference to any reservations or understandings that may have been maintained by particular states.

The substantive criminal law The effect of these extensive definitional provisions is taken even further in the Elements of Crimes, adopted in 2000.[39] For the most part these follow precisely the language of the Statute itself, or elaborate on it in reasonable and predictable ways. But it is impossible to elaborate on statutory texts without taking positions on their meaning. On particular points it seems that the Elements of Crimes are more restrictive than equivalent interpretations given to parallel provisions of the ICTY and ICTR Statutes by the *ad hoc* tribunals. What matters for present purposes, however, is the detail and depth with which the Statute autonomously defines the three crimes which fall immediately within its jurisdiction.

Moreover, experience suggests that these definitions will be applied internally as well as internationally. In

[39] UN Doc. PCNICC/2000/1/Add.2.

order to take full advantage of the principle of complementarity, it will be logical for states implementing the Rome Statute to transpose these new definitions of crimes into their own legal systems. Indeed, this has already been done, for example, in the United Kingdom and Australian implementing legislation.[40] Thus the international criminal justice system of the Rome Statute will tend to surpass existing treaty provisions defining the same crimes, at both the international and the national level.

The outcome: the ICC under the Rome Statute

As a result of these drafting developments, the International Criminal Court under the Rome Statute is a distinct and to a considerable extent an autonomous criminal justice system for the investigation and prosecution of a small number of serious international crimes. In relation to such crimes, the values associated with the idea of a criminal justice

---

40 United Kingdom, International Criminal Court Act 2001, Part 5, 'Offences Under Domestic Law'; Australia, International Criminal Court (Consequential Amendments) Act 2002, Act No. 42 of 2002, Schedule 1, 'Amendment of the Criminal Code Act 1995'.

system have largely prevailed over those foreign relations perspectives according to which the ICC was to be a stop-gap criminal trial process only for special cases. That is testament both to the power of the ICC drafting process, and also to a certain risk being taken, in particular *vis-à-vis* third states.

No doubt the idea of the ICC as a supplementary process remains. The principle of complementarity is prominent, even if it is no longer an element in terms of the ICC's underlying jurisdiction. Applied as intended, it will give priority to states (whether or not parties to the Statute) which are willing and able to investigate allegations of crimes for themselves. Greater difficulties may arise where a state (whether or not a party) refuses to conduct its own investigation, because it takes a different view of the facts or a narrower view of the alleged crime or for some other reason. It may be said that this is the point of having an ICC in the first place. But since it is for the investigating authority to determine for itself the scope of the crime being investigated, once again the relative autonomy of ICC processes is demonstrated. It remains to be seen how the dynamic potential for action by the Prosecutor, and reaction by states, will be played out.

At the same time, the limited subject-matter jurisdiction of the Court (a function of the automaticity of its jurisdiction over the three crimes) risks producing the situation that very serious crimes of international concern cannot be addressed. The Lockerbie prosecution, a matter of international concern if ever there was one, would fall outside the Court's jurisdiction, even though the ILC regarded it as (in future) the type-case of a situation appropriate for the Court. As to more recent events, it is far from clear that the World Trade Center bombings of 11 September 2001 could have been brought within the ICC's subject-matter jurisdiction – presumably only under the rubric of a crime against humanity. We have seen in other fora how the availability of jurisdiction over genocide has tended to lead to arguments for a broader interpretation of the definition of genocide. The same is likely to happen for other crimes within the jurisdiction of the Court. It remains to be seen whether the Elements of Crimes will provide the intended stability of the definitions of crimes, when we are faced with new situations involving large-scale terrorism or violence in internal armed conflict.

5

Prospects and issues for the International Criminal Court: lessons from Yugoslavia and Rwanda

CHERIE BOOTH

The Rome Statute of the ICC has its flaws – the nature of the drafting process and the political issues at stake ensured that – but we have now reached a stage where the principle of individual criminal liability is established for those responsible for the most serious crimes, and where an institution has been established – on a permanent basis – to ensure the punishment of such individuals. The Court, no doubt, will serve as a painful reminder of the atrocities of the past century and the level to which humanity can stoop. I say nothing new when I tell you that it appears we are doomed to repeat history. As Judge Richard Goldstone, former Chief Prosecutor at The Hague Tribunals, has wryly commented: 'The hope of "never again" became the reality of again and again.'[1] But

[1] 'Were They Just Obeying Orders?', *Guardian*, 7 May 1996, p. 10, quoted in Simon Chesterman, 'Never Again ... and Again: Law, Order, and the Gender of War Crimes in Bosnia and Beyond' (1997) 22 *Yale Journal of International Law* 299 at 316.

at the same time I am convinced that the International Criminal Court, with independent prosecutors putting tyrants and torturers in the dock before independent judges, reflects a post-war aspiration come true.

Professor James Crawford spoke about the work of the UN International Law Commission in preparing the Draft Statute of the ICC, and the transformation of that draft into the final Statute as it emerged at Rome in the summer of 1998.[2] During the time that Professor Crawford and his colleagues in the Commission were considering the Draft Statute, events compelled the creation of an international criminal tribunal on an *ad hoc* basis to respond to the atrocities that were being committed in the territory of the former Yugoslavia. That tribunal, the International Criminal Tribunal for the former Yugoslavia, was established by the Security Council in 1993 and mandated to prosecute persons responsible for serious violations of international humanitarian law committed in the territory of the former Yugoslavia since 1991. Then, in November 1994, and acting on a request from Rwanda, the Security Council voted to create a second *ad hoc* tribunal, charged with the prosecution of genocide and other serious violations of international humanitarian law, commit-

[2]   See chapter 4 above.

ted in Rwanda and in neighbouring countries during the year 1994. These two Tribunals – the first international criminal tribunals since Nuremberg – are close relatives, sharing virtually identical statutes, as well as the same Prosecutor and Appeals Chamber. Most significantly, both share the same overall blue-print for international criminal justice: an international criminal forum applying rules of international law, staffed by independent prosecutors and judges, holding persons individually responsible for crimes against humanity and war crimes, after allowing them a fair trial.

The Rwanda and Yugoslav Tribunals provided the strongest support for the idea that a permanent international criminal court was desirable and practical. The Statutes of the ICTY and ICTR influenced the emerging Draft Statute that the ILC was drawing up under Professor Crawford's direction. And, by the time delegates convened in Rome in June 1998 to draft a statute for a permanent international criminal court, the Tribunals provided a working model of what might be possible. In addition, the jurisprudence of The Hague Tribunals – for example, the progressive view that crimes against humanity could be committed in peace-time, and the decision that war crimes could be committed during an internal armed conflict – contributed to the debates in Rome and eventually came to be reflected in the Rome Statute.

The Statute of the International Criminal Court was adopted on 17 July 1998 by an overwhelming majority of the states attending the Rome Conference. To date, the Rome Statute has been signed by 139 states and sixty-seven states have ratified it. One significant absentee as a ratifier is the United States, but I am pleased to say that it has not followed through on the reported threat that the US would remove its signature to the Statute, one of President Clinton's final acts in office in December 2000. It is notable that, within just four years, the treaty has achieved the sixty required ratifications, far sooner than was generally expected. The Statute will enter into force on 1 July 2002, at which time the Court's jurisdiction over genocide, war crimes and crimes against humanity will take effect. The Assembly of States Parties will meet for the first time in September 2002. I need hardly mention that the opposition to the Court displayed by the United States – in particular its decision to oppose the adoption of the Statute at Rome – has dampened the excitement that goes along with these developments. With or without the involvement of that country, however, the Court will be up and running within the next year.

What are its prospects? The answer to that question might be found, at least partly, in the experience of the ICTY and the ICTR. So, by reference to the experience of the ICTY and the ICTR, I should like to address the prospects of the ICC in relation to three issues: first, the prospects in relation to the legitimacy and credibility of the Court; secondly, the prospects insofar as the Court's functions are concerned; and, thirdly, the prospects for the Court as a truly 'international' institution.

Prospects for credibility and legitimacy: the International Criminal Court and women

We are not far away from having to make decisions about the appointment of judges to the International Criminal Court. The period for submitting nominations began at the first meeting of the Assembly of States Parties in September 2002 with the close of the nomination period in December 2002. Elections will take place during the second meeting of the Assembly of States Parties, in January 2003, in time for the Court's opening in March 2003.

The prospects for an effective, legitimate and credible Court depend, to a very great extent, on the composition of its bench. It is of singular importance that the Court be composed of judges with the most appropriate qualifications, as the Statute requires. That means, among other points, that there be representation of the principal legal systems and appropriate geographical representation, and that there be an appropriate gender balance.

Article 36 of the Rome Statute, concerning qualification of judges, requires that there be 'fair representation of female and male judges'.[3] This is the very first time that the statute of any international court – and there are now more than thirty – establishes this requirement. It is an important development. How many of these eighteen judges should be women, to satisfy the condition of 'fair representation'? That is a contentious issue. But one thing is clear – the Rome Statute recognises the need to change the international *status quo*. The international judiciary is overwhelmingly male, suggesting that the selection process operates within unacceptable limits. A study prepared by Jan Linehan last year for the Project on International Courts and Tribunals shows that, of 153 judges attached to the nine principal international courts, just eighteen were women.[4] This is partly because women are under-represented as judges in most national legal systems, as well as under-represented at the international level. However, it is not credible to suggest that under-representation is due to a

---

[3]   Article 36(8)(a)(iii).

[4]   See Cherie Booth and Philippe Sands, 'Keep Politics out of the Global Courts', *Guardian*, 13 July 2001.

dearth of suitably qualified candidates. Other factors include the selection process itself, with the lack of priority that states attach to the issue, and persistent ideas about the nature of suitable candidates. Many states, for instance, persist in promoting a particular type of candidate – one with a background in academia, diplomacy and the International Law Commission – to which women are less likely to conform. It is vital, however, that the appointment of women to the International Criminal Court be taken seriously by all states parties to the Rome Statute. The under-representation of women on the Court threatens to undermine the legitimacy and authority of the institution from day one, and, as the Court grows and becomes involved in high-profile cases, it will be crucial that international criminal justice be seen to be fair and representative of international society as a whole.

The need for female appointees to the Court is reinforced by the attention given by the ICC Statute to women's issues, as compared with the very limited concern that women's issues have received in international criminal law in the past.[5] In the field of armed conflict, history is replete with examples of women

5   See generally Rhonda Copelon, 'Gender Crimes as War Crimes: Integrating Crimes Against Women into International Criminal Law' (2000) 46 *McGill Law Journal* 217 at 220–8.

being targeted as victims of sexual assault as part of a policy of war. Rape and other acts of sexual violence have long been utilised as instruments of warfare, used not only as an attack on the individual victim but also as a means to 'humiliate, shame, degrade and terrify the entire ... group'.[6] These victims have been let down when it has come to the prevention and prosecution of these offences, largely because sexual violence has been regarded as an accepted concomitant of war, even if it was not explicitly condoned. The story is told of the Byzantine emperor Alexius who, in appealing for recruits during the First Crusade, extolled the beauty of Greek women as an incentive to go to war, an idea which later came to be known as that of 'booty and beauty', and which was associated with success in battle. More recently, General Patton's writings about the Second World War in his book entitled *War As I Knew It* reflect the 'inevitability' of rape in times of war. Patton remembers:

> I then told him that, in spite of my most diligent efforts, there would unquestionably be some

6   See Theodore Meron, 'Rape as a Crime Under International Humanitarian Law' (1993) 87 *American Journal of International Law* 424 at 425, citing Tadeusz Mazowiecki, Special Rapporteur, 'Report on the Situation of Human Rights in the Territory of the Former Yugoslavia', UN Doc. A/48/92 and S/25341, Annex, pp. 20 and 57 (1993).

> raping, and that I should like to have the details as
> early as possible so that the offenders can be
> properly hanged.[7]

And, of course, besides the concomitant *inevitability* of sexual violence, rape has historically served a tactical function in war as an expression of the totality of victory – a sort of 'sexual *coup de grâce*'. As the events in Rwanda and the former Yugoslavia so horribly remind us, this function of sexual aggression against women often serves as a grotesque public display of domination where the 'rape of the woman's body symbolically represents the rape of the community itself'.[8]

At the international level it was only in relatively recent times that sexual violence against women in armed conflict came to be regarded as an important issue, in serious need of redress. Since 1990, international criminal law has made greater progress on women's issues than during any other time in recorded history. The Rome Statute both exemplifies the progress

---

[7] George S. Patton, *War As I Knew It* (1947), p. 23, quoted in Susan Brownmiller, *Against Our Will: Men, Women and Rape* (1975), p. 23, and cited in Simon Chesterman, 'Never Again … and Again: Law, Order, and the Gender of War Crimes in Bosnia and Beyond' (1997) 22 *Yale Journal of International Law* 299 at 324.

[8] Simon Chesterman, 'Never Again … and Again: Law, Order, and the Gender of War Crimes in Bosnia and Beyond' (1997) 22 *Yale Journal of International Law* 299 at 328.

thus far and hints at the future contribution that the Court can make to the attainment of justice for women. The Statute allows for prosecution of a wide range of gender-based or sex-based crimes, provides certain protections to victims of these crimes, and calls for the inclusion of women in the different organs of the Court. The inclusion of these gender provisions in the Rome Statute clearly did not occur in a vacuum. The fact that the Statute is progressive with regard to women's issues is in no small measure due to the struggle of civil society and the women's human rights movement, including in the Rome negotiations. Furthermore, by the time the delegates convened in Rome to draft the Statute, they had the benefit of drawing on the jurisprudence that the ICTY and the ICTR had developed as regards the substantive elements of gender and sex crimes, as well as on the Tribunals' experience in the investigation, prosecution and adjudication of such crimes.

As we stand on the eve of appointing judges to the ICC, one of the most important lessons we can draw from the ICTY and ICTR is that there are advantages that women judges bring to the bench when it comes to the prosecution of gender-based and sex-based crimes. The UN Secretary-General's Report that accompanied the Statute of the ICTY recognised as much by providing that, given the nature of the crimes committed and the sensitivities of victims of rape and sexual assault, due consideration needed to be given to the employment of qualified women to the Tribunal's staff.[9] And, as an example of the contribution that women judges have made in cases involving sexual violence, consider the decision of the Rwanda Tribunal in the *Akayesu* case.[10]

Akayesu was the first case heard before the Rwanda Tribunal, and is heralded today as possibly 'the most important decision rendered thus far in the history of women's jurisprudence'.[11] Not only was it the first international war crimes trial in history to try and convict a defendant for genocide, it was also the first judgment in which an accused has been found guilty of genocide for crimes which expressly included sexualised violence, and the first time that an accused has been found guilty of rape as a crime against humanity. But the obvious

---

[9] See Report of the Secretary-General, UN Doc. S/25704, 3 May 1993, cited in Cate Steains, 'Gender Issues', in Roy Lee (ed.), *The International Criminal Court: The Making of the Rome Statute: Issues, Negotiations, Results* (Kluwer Law International, The Hague, 1999), p. 376.

[10] Case No. ICTR-96-4-T, Judgment, ICTR Trial Chamber, 2 September 1998, available at www.ictr.org.

[11] See Kelly Askin, 'Women's Issues in International Criminal Law: Recent Developments and the Potential Contribution of the ICC', in Dinah Shelton (ed.), *International Crimes, Peace, and Human Rights: The Role of the International Criminal Court* (Transnational Publishers, Ardsley, NY, 2000), p. 52.

contribution this judgment makes to the advancement of gender issues might not have come about, were it not for the intervention of Judge Pillay, a South African Indian, and the only female judge on the Rwandan Tribunal at the time.

It was February 1997 and the trial had just begun. Jean-Paul Akayesu was in the dock. He had been charged with giving orders for, and participating in, crimes against humanity committed at the Taba Commune. Surprisingly, given what we now know of the Rwandan situation, no charges or evidence of rape were initially brought at the trial, with the prosecutor claiming that it was impossible to document rape because women would not talk about it.[12] However, Judge Pillay delicately pursued a line of inquiry with two women – called by the

12   See Rhonda Copelon, 'Gender Crimes as War Crimes:
     Integrating Crimes Against Women into International Criminal
     Law' (2000) 46 *McGill Law Journal* 217 at 224–5. Copelon points
     out that rape formed no part of the first series of the ICTR
     indictments, even though it was included as a crime against
     humanity in the ICTR Statute and mentioned therein as an
     example of the war crime of humiliating and degrading treat-
     ment. This was notwithstanding the fact that a Human Rights
     Watch/Fédération Internationale des Ligues des Droits de
     l'Homme report focused on rape and sexual assault in the Taba
     Commune, over which Jean Paul Akayesu had control. The same
     report documented the failure of the prosecutorial staff to take
     rape seriously, as well as the inappropriateness and lack of train-
     ing of the investigative staff to undertake rape enquiries.

Prosecutor to testify to *other* crimes – as to whether rape had occurred in the Commune. The first witness explained how she had fled her village before the slaughter began and had managed to hide in a tree, where she stayed for several days. After deciding it was safe, she climbed down to discover that only her 6-year-old daughter had survived a massacre in which the rest of her family was killed. Together they tried to escape the area but were caught by Hutus and her daughter was gang-raped. Her sworn statement taken before the trial mirrored this evidence given in court about the murders, but was silent about the details of her daughter's rape, apparently because the investigators had not asked her about rape. After further careful examination by Judge Pillay, the witness also testified that she had heard that young girls were raped at the Taba Commune, where Akayesu was in charge. The second witness confirmed this. She testified that she had been taken into custody and held at the Bureau where Akayesu had stood and watched as girls were dragged into the compound and repeatedly raped by armed militia. Commenting on this situation, Judge Pillay said:

> We have to try a case before us where this person [Akayesu] has not been specifically charged with rape. We're hearing the evidence, but the defence counsel has not cross-examined the witnesses who

gave testimony of sexual violence, because it is not in the indictment. I'm extremely dismayed that we're hearing evidence of rape and sexual violence against women and children, yet it is not in the indictments because the witnesses were never asked about it.[13]

The consequence was that, in June 1997, the indictment was amended by the Prosecutor to add charges of sexual violence. But many agree that such additional charges would not have come about, had it not been for the instrumental role Judge Pillay played in questioning witnesses and evoking testimony of gross sexual violence.[14] When the trial resumed, extensive testimony concerning rape and other forms of sexual violence was

[13] Jan Goodwin, 'Rwanda: Justice Denied', (1997) 6 *On the Issues*, No. 4, at 2, available at http://www.echonyc.com/~onissues/ f97rwanda.html.

[14] See Cate Steains, 'Gender Issues', in Roy Lee (ed.), *The International Criminal Court: The Making of the Rome Statute: Issues, Negotiations, Results* (Kluwer Law International, The Hague, 1999), p. 378, as well as Rhonda Copelon, 'Gender Crimes as War Crimes: Integrating Crimes Against Women into International Criminal Law' (2000) 46 *McGill Law Journal* 217 at 224–6. See also Kelly Askin, who writes that 'it is highly unlikely that the *Akayesu* decision ... which exemplifies a heightened awareness of crimes committed against women, would have demonstrated such gender sensitivity without South African Judge Navanethem Pillay's participation in both the trial and the judgment': Kelly Askin, 'Sexual Violence in Decisions and Indictments of the Yugoslav and Rwandan Tribunals: Current Status' (1999) 93 *American Journal of*

admitted into evidence – evidence that was used to establish that sexual violence was an integral part of the genocide committed during the Rwandan conflict.[15] The *Akayesu* matter stands out, therefore, as a reminder that, when it comes to the issue of composition of international criminal courts, the ultimate beneficiaries of a 'fair representation of female judges' on the bench are the victims of sexual violence themselves.

In relation then to the specific nature of sex-based and gender-based offences in the Rome Statute, the 'fair representation' of female judges goes beyond the issue of gender equality. The lessons from the Rwandan and Yugoslav Tribunals make it clear that the presence of female judges, as well as of women in senior positions in the Prosecutor's office, would contribute significantly to the effective prosecution of sexual violence against women. As Judge Pillay, now President of the Rwanda Tribunal, has recently stressed, in this new field of international criminal justice, '[w]ho interprets the law

International Law 97 at 98, n. 8; see also Barbara Bedont and Katherine Martinez, 'Ending Impunity for Gender Crimes under the International Criminal Court' (1999) 6 *Brown Journal of World Affairs* 65–85, available at www.crlp.org/pub_art_ icc.html.

[15] See Kelly Askin, 'Sexual Violence in Decisions and Indictments of the Yugoslav and Rwandan Tribunals: Current Status' (1999) 93 *American Journal of International Law* 97 at 105–6.

is at least as important as who makes the law, if not more so'.[16]

The requirement of 'fair representation' is not the only requirement that has potential consequences for women under the Rome Statute. In addition to 'fair representation' of female judges, the Statute provides that judges with legal expertise on specific issues, 'including, but not limited to, violence against women or children, ought to be appointed'.[17] This is a commendable provision in light of perceived challenges to judges' impartiality on account of their specialist backgrounds. One such challenge is illustrated by the decision of the Yugoslav Tribunal in *Prosecutor* v. *Furundzija*.[18]

The culture of impunity for sexual crimes that preceded the establishment of the ICTY made it essential to declare that rape or other forms of sexual

[16] United Nations, Division for the Advancement of Women and Centre for Refugee Studies, York University, Canada, 'Gender-Based Prosecution: Report of the Expert Group Meeting', EGM/GBP/1997/Report, Toronto, 9–12 November 1997, p. 33, cited in Barbara Bedont and Katherine Martinez, 'Ending Impunity for Gender Crimes under the International Criminal Court' (1999) 6 *Brown Journal of World Affairs* 65–85, available at www.crlp.org/pub_art_icc.html.

[17] ICC Statute, Article 38(8)(b).

[18] See *Prosecutor* v. *Furundzija*, Case No. IT-95-17/1-T, Judgment, ICTY Trial Chamber II, 10 December 1998, available at http://www.un.org/icty/furundzija/trialc2/judgement/index.htm.

violence, even if committed against just one victim, are serious violations of international humanitarian law.[19] The *Furundzija* case involved the multiple rapes of one woman by a single physical perpetrator during one day of the Yugoslav conflict. For the Prosecutors, the case was an opportunity to show that an accused could be tried exclusively for sexual violence against a single victim, notwithstanding the limited resources of the Tribunal and the difficulties in justifying such a prosecution in the light of other serious violations (committed against multiple victims) that had taken place in Yugoslavia. The eleven-day trial – the shortest held to date in the ICTY – confirms that a single instance of sexual violence committed in the context of an armed conflict warrants prosecution as a war crime. Besides its normative value as a condemnation of random, isolated rape, committed simply because the 'fog of war' creates the opportunity to do so, the case also creates a precedent for courts martial and other domestic courts to punish such acts as war crimes.[20]

---

[19] See generally Kelly Askin, 'Women's Issues in International Criminal Law: Recent Developments and the Potential Contribution of the ICC', in Dinah Shelton (ed.), *International Crimes, Peace, and Human Rights: The Role of the International Criminal Court* (Transnational Publishers, Ardsley, NY, 2000), p. 55.

[20] *Ibid.*, p. 56.

However, unhappy with the outcome of the case, Furundzija's lawyers sought to overturn the ruling by having the Presiding Judge, Florence Mumba, disqualified for failing to disclose that she had previously served as a member of the UN's Commission on the Status of Women. In the words of one commentator, the defence 'clearly insinuated that women judges, particularly women who have attempted to redress human rights violations against women, cannot be impartial because they are predisposed to promote a feminist agenda, and therefore should be recused from adjudicating any cases involving crimes against women'.[21] It was indeed true that Florence Mumba had been a member of the Commission on the Status of Women between 1992 and 1995 (the ICTY's Public Information Service and Yearbook confirmed as much!), and during that time the Commission had issued a resolution condemning the sexual violence taking place in Yugoslavia, urging the prosecution to seek justice for these victims, and pressing for a broad definition of war-time rape. To the defence, however, this meant that Judge Mumba should have been disqualified for having advanced in the judgment a 'legal and political agenda' that she had helped create as a member of the Commission.[22]

[21] *Ibid.*
[22] See ICTY Appeals Chamber, *Prosecutor* v. *Furundzija*, Case No.

The Appeal Chamber dismissed the application. It ruled that, in the circumstances of the case, a 'fair-minded and informed member of the public' could not reasonably apprehend bias on the part of Judge Mumba.[23] It goes without saying, I think, that all persons – even lawyers – have histories, specialisations and philosophies, but, equally so, appointment to the bench carries with it recognition of the moral and intellectual integrity of the individual, to put aside background factors and to act as impartially and independently as possible as an arbiter of fact and law. There is no good reason to believe that this hallmark of judicial office is undermined by the appointment of judges who specialise in an area of law or who have written or spoken advocating certain legal or philosophical opinions. Because of the various gender-based and sex-based crimes in the Rome Statute it is important that women (and men) with specialist expertise regarding violence against women be appointed to the Court. By expressly stipulating that judges with legal expertise on issues such as violence against women ought to be appointed, the

IT-95-17/1-A, 21 July 2000, paras 25 and 169–70, available at http://www.un.org/icty/furundzija/appeal/judgement/index.ht m.

[23] See ICTY Appeals Chamber, *Prosecutor* v. *Furundzija*, appended declaration of Judge Shahabuddeen, available at http://www.un.org/icty/furundzija/appeal/judgement/index.htm.

Rome Statute appropriately acknowledges that expertise in a particular area is beneficial. It also makes it clear that there is no presumption of bias or predisposition of experts to rule a certain way, be they male or female.[24]

I therefore welcome the Rome Statute's express requirement that there be a fair representation between the sexes on the ICC's bench, and express the hope that all states parties will take that requirement seriously when they nominate candidates and when they exercise their right to vote for particular candidates.

Prospects for criminal justice: what role for the International Criminal Court?

Naturally, the question of justice for women in the international criminal law field is only a small part of a much larger question, namely, what do we understand by the phrase 'international criminal justice' itself? In relation to the ICC, let us consider some of the functions we expect the Court to perform, and assess its prospects in

[24] See Kelly Askin, 'Women's Issues in International Criminal Law: Recent Developments and the Potential Contribution of the ICC', in Dinah Shelton (ed.), *International Crimes, Peace, and Human Rights: The Role of the International Criminal Court* (Transnational Publishers, Ardsley, NY, 2000), p. 62.

relation to those functions. The experience of The Hague and Arusha Tribunals, and of Nuremberg before that, shows that the ICC will have an effect beyond the trials themselves, and significance beyond traditional conceptions of justice. While one leading commentator in the field rightly reminds us that 'it is important to be modest about the potential of war crimes trials and international criminal law generally',[25] modesty or realism when it comes to the International Criminal Court need not be cynicism.

The International Criminal Court as a public demonstration of justice

The International Criminal Court is a call to responsibility for persons guilty of 'the most serious crimes of concern to the international community as a whole'.[26] In this respect, it takes seriously the words of Justice Robert Jackson, Chief Prosecutor at Nuremberg, who famously said that letting major war criminals live undisturbed to write their 'memoirs' in peace 'would

[25] See Gerry Simpson, 'War Crimes: A Critical Introduction', in Timothy McCormack and Gerry Simpson (eds.), *The Law of War Crimes: National and International Approaches* (Kluwer Law International, London and The Hague, 1997), p. 1 at p. 29.

[26] See the Preamble to the Statute of the International Criminal Court.

mock the dead and make cynics of the living'.[27] Perhaps the function of a trial in the International Criminal Court is thus first and foremost a proclamation that certain conduct is unacceptable to the world community. That may sound like an obvious statement, but it is not one which international law has always embraced. While war crimes are committed every day and whole races have been defined by their experience of genocide or crimes against humanity, international laws designed to punish these acts have only been invoked when there has existed 'an unusually propitious constellation of political factors'.[28] In the twentieth century, such a constellation of factors led only to the trials at Nuremberg and Tokyo after the Second World War, and, in the 1990s, to the creation of The Hague and Arusha Tribunals – a selective outpouring of indignation at best, and an insidious message at the international level that, to a large degree, war crimes and crimes against humanity are followed by impunity.

The International Criminal Court presents itself as the mechanism to cure this defect in the international

[27] Robert H. Jackson, *The Nurnberg Case, as Presented by Robert H. Jackson* (1947), p. 8.

[28] Gerry Simpson, 'War Crimes: A Critical Introduction', in Timothy McCormack and Gerry Simpson (eds.), *The Law of War Crimes: National and International Approaches* (Kluwer Law International, London and The Hague, 1997), p. 1 at p. 28.

legal system by providing a public demonstration of justice. The act of punishing particular individuals – whether the leaders, or star generals, or foot soldiers – becomes an instrument through which individual accountability for massive human rights violations is increasingly internalised as part of the fabric of our international society. At the same time, it is a method by which we put a stop to the culture of impunity that has taken hold at the international level. Former Secretary of State Warren Christopher suggested in the context of the Balkan crisis that '[b]old tyrants and fearful minorities are watching to see whether ethnic cleansing is a policy the world will tolerate'. To him, '[i]f we hope to promote the spread of freedom, or we hope to encourage the emergence of peaceful, multi-ethnic democracies, our answers must be a resounding "no"'.[29] The ICC, building on the work done by The Hague and Arusha Tribunals, is the means by which a resounding 'no' is now possible in respect of every crime set out in the Rome Statute. In that regard, it is of singular importance to note that no one – not even a serving head of

[29] Provisional Verbatim Record of the Three Thousand One Hundred and Seventy-Fifth Meeting, UN SCOR, 3175th mtg, pp. 12–13, UN Doc. S/PV.3175, 22 February 1993, quoted in Payam Akhavan, 'Justice in The Hague, Peace in the Former Yugoslavia? A Commentary on the United Nations War Crimes Tribunal' (1998) 20 *Human Rights Quarterly* 737 at 750.

state – will be able to claim immunity from the jurisdiction of the Court.

Upholding the rule of law: the creation of order

Besides the moral condemnation of these crimes at the international level, the ICC will serve a second, and vital, purpose, namely, upholding the rule of law. To respond to mass atrocity with legal prosecution is to exact retribution by embracing legal order. The retributive theme was evident most clearly in the Allies' prosecution of Nazis at Nuremberg after affirming, earlier in the war, their commitment to prosecute the war 'criminals' for their 'acts of savagery'.[30] In the closing days of the Second World War it was far from clear that the Allies would carry through with this legal commitment; the British Prime Minister, for example, is widely reported as having favoured the summary execution of a dozen or so leading members of the Nazi hierarchy. However, in the end, Nuremberg's legacy is that of legal retribution – of staying the hand of vengeance and of ceding 'Power … to Reason'.[31]

[30] See Simon Chesterman, 'Never Again … and Again: Law, Order, and the Gender of War Crimes in Bosnia and Beyond' (1997) 22 *Yale Journal of International Law* 299 at 312.

[31] See Robert H. Jackson, *The Nürnberg Case, as Presented by Robert H. Jackson* (1947), p. 94.

Is retribution in the classic sense what the International Criminal Court is meant to achieve? In part, the answer is 'yes', as evidenced by the Preamble to the Rome Statute which proclaims that 'the most serious crimes of concern to the international community as a whole must not go unpunished and that their effective prosecution must be ensured'. Of course, retribution as a motivating force comes with its own problems. One of these problems is that a war crimes trial is an exercise in partial justice, to the extent that it reminds us that the majority of war crimes go unpunished.[32] This, many of you will recall, was a criticism in particular of the Yugoslavia Tribunal's decision to prosecute Dusko Tadic – a mere foot soldier in the events of the Balkan crisis – simply because it did not have custody of a higher ranking, more significant figure. It was argued that there were hundreds more like Tadic, and that there was little point in convicting one among them in what seemed to have been a mere lottery. We can expect that the International Criminal Court will face similar challenges if 'situations' involving mass atrocities are referred to it for prosecution. However, given the nature

---

[32] Gerry Simpson, 'War Crimes: A Critical Introduction', in Timothy McCormack and Gerry Simpson (eds.), *The Law of War Crimes: National and International Approaches* (Kluwer Law International, London and The Hague, 1997), p. 1 at p. 8.

of mass atrocities such as those committed in Rwanda and Yugoslavia, it will be nearly impossible for the Prosecutor to avoid making broader strategic choices when it comes to deciding whom to prosecute. We should draw some solace, I would suggest, from the fact that, in a world in which a multitude of people may have become embroiled in war crimes, the punishment of each and every offender is not necessary to achieve respect for the rule of law, or to declare our disgust at the acts committed. Moreover, as Andrew Clapham and Philippe Sands described in earlier lectures, the role of the ICC will be complementary to that of national courts, and we can expect national criminal justice to play an equally important role to the ICC. As was written in relation to the experience at Nuremberg, '[t]he purpose was not to punish all cases of criminal guilt … The exemplary punishments served the purpose of restoring the legal order, that is of reassuring the whole community that what they had witnessed for so many years was criminal behaviour.'[33]

---

[33] Bert Röling, 'Aspects of Criminal Responsibility for Violations of Laws of War', in Antonio Cassese (ed.), *The New Humanitarian Law of Armed Conflict* (Editoriale Scientifica, Naples, 1979), p. 206.

Memory against forgetting:[34] *the ICC as truth-teller*

The third function of an ICC trial – and closely aligned with the value of upholding the rule of law – is the opportunity it creates for truth telling. Truth, after all, is the cornerstone of the rule of law. Two important points, I think, need to be kept in mind. The first is that international criminal trials have a commemorative potential; they can build an objective and impartial record of events.[35] This was true of Nuremberg, and it is true also in respect of the current trials in The Hague. Naturally, we should recognise the tension between the production of history and the task of conducting a criminal trial. A criminal trial, with its elaborate rules regarding relevance and admissibility of evidence as well as its focus on the accused in court, means that it can never provide a definitive and comprehensive record of history. The ICC is able to provide a coherent and judicially manageable account of tragic events, a

---

[34] The renowned Czech author, Milan Kundera, reminds us that 'the struggle of man over power is the struggle of memory over forgetting'.

[35] Antonio Cassese, 'On the Current Trends Towards Criminal Prosecution and Punishment of Breaches of International Humanitarian Law' (1998) 9 *European Journal of International Law* 2 at 14, available at http://www.ejil.org/journal/Vol9/No1/art1.html.

'judicial truth', if you will. But the painting of the fuller picture of history, through local initiatives such as truth commissions based on popular participation, must be left to those affected by the crimes.[36] That having been said, we can rest assured that the materials collected by the ICC which have passed its strict rules of admissibility of evidence can contribute to the creation of objective accounts of events which will play an important role in fighting forgetting.

The second important point is this: proceedings before the ICC have the potential of countering the attribution of collective responsibility for acts committed by individuals. Richard Goldstone put it well when commenting on the emotive photographs of the accused in the dock at Nuremberg. He said that 'one sees a group of criminals. One does not see a group of representatives of the German people – the people who produced Goethe or Heine or Beethoven.' As he put it: 'The Nuremberg Trials were a meaningful instrument for avoiding the guilt of the Nazis being ascribed to the whole German people.'[37] That this is an important function for the ICC can be seen

---

[36] See Payam Akhavan, 'Justice in The Hague, Peace in the Former Yugoslavia? A Commentary on the United Nations War Crimes Tribunal' (1998) 20 *Human Rights Quarterly* 737 at 784.

[37] Richard Goldstone, 'Fifty Years After Nuremberg: A New International Criminal Tribunal for Human Rights Criminals', in Albert Jongman (ed.), *Contemporary Genocides: Causes,*

from the experience of the ethnic violence in Rwanda and Yugoslavia. The truth telling of The Hague Tribunals has been essential in the promotion of reconciliation by individualising the guilt of hateful leaders and disabusing people of the myth that adversary ethnic groups bear collective responsibility for crimes.

The *international* International Criminal Court

Thus far, I have considered some of the functions of the ICC in its pursuit of 'international criminal justice'. I would like to conclude this lecture by focusing on the *international* aspirations of the ICC when it comes to criminal justice. International lawyers will point to a conceptual problem associated with the vision of international criminality that arises because of the structure of the international legal system itself.[38] The idea of an

Cases, Consequences (Leiden, 1996), p. 215, cited in Payam Akhavan, 'Justice in The Hague, Peace in the Former Yugoslavia? A Commentary on the United Nations War Crimes Tribunal' (1998) 20 *Human Rights Quarterly* 737 at 766.

[38] See generally Gerry Simpson, 'War Crimes: A Critical Introduction', in Timothy McCormack and Gerry Simpson (eds.), *The Law of War Crimes: National and International Approaches* (Kluwer Law International, London and The Hague, 1997), p. 1 at pp. 16–17.

international criminal law – involving a public law dimension with an underlying system of shared social ethics – seems strangely inappropriate, given that the international regime has no central sovereign and is morally pluralistic.

This conceptual difficulty associated with international criminality has been overcome, however, by endorsing the idea that there is an international social system which is realised in a number of ways, including the very notion of an International Criminal Court. The second half of the twentieth century has seen the strengthening of human rights and of the humanitarian law of war and the growing sense that, because individuals live under the international legal system, they must necessarily have rights and obligations flowing from it. The fact that delegates at Rome were able to come together and finalise the ICC Statute is evidence of the existence of a social system built on universal respect for the idea of human rights – a system which denounces the most serious war crimes and crimes against humanity because of a recognition that tolerating such atrocities diminishes and threatens everyone.

The prospects for the ICC as a protectorate of the ideals of the international community as a whole become difficult to imagine, however, when some states elect to exclude themselves from that vision. This is particularly true when those states are powerful, and strikingly so when such powerful states, like the United States, are traditionally associated with the very values the ICC seeks to endorse.

From its earliest beginnings, an important element of the US conception of its own national interest has been the development and maintenance of an international rule of law. The importance the Framers gave to international law is reflected in the Constitution itself, whereby Congress is given power to 'define and punish Piracies and Felonies committed on the high seas, and Offences against the Law of Nations'.[39] In the last century the US was a leading force in the establishment of the Permanent Court of Arbitration; a chief architect of the United Nations, the IMF and the World Bank; a leading sponsor of the *ad hoc* tribunals on Rwanda and the former Yugoslavia; and a vocal endorser of the idea of an international criminal court. Indeed, President Clinton called for a permanent war crimes tribunal shortly before the Rome Conference, when addressing genocide survivors in Rwanda.[40] The impact of the US

[39] Constitution of the United States, Article I, Section 8.
[40] During March 1998, at Kigali. See Lawrence Weschler, 'Exceptional Cases in Rome: The United States and the Struggle for an ICC', in Sarah Sewall and Carl Kaysen (eds.), *The United States and the International Criminal Court* (Rowman & Littlefield, Lanham, MD and Oxford, 2000), p. 91.

failure to support the ICC may be symbolically important – a high-profile rejection of a major initiative for
the rule of law in international affairs. But it will also be
a lost opportunity if a state with a long-standing
commitment to human rights does not take a lead in
shaping the work of the world's first international
criminal court. Indeed, the ICC Statute has principles
central to American conceptions of justice all over it,
reflecting ideas such as due process, command responsibility and superior orders, to name but a few.[41]
Participation in the ICC would mean that the US would
have a major role in shaping the evolution of the Court
in ways that further this vision of the future of the international legal system.

At the Rome Conference in 1998, the US worked
closely with the UK throughout long and difficult negotiations to ensure that the Statute of the ICC contains
adequate safeguards against politically motivated
prosecutions of our citizens. It is plain that the UK was
and remains satisfied that this was achieved.

Now, as then, the UK remains convinced that US and

[41] See the comments of Theodore Meron, recorded in Lawrence
Weschler, 'Exceptional Cases in Rome: The United States and the
Struggle for an ICC', in Sarah Sewall and Carl Kaysen (eds.), *The
United States and the International Criminal Court* (Rowman &
Littlefield, Lanham, MD and Oxford, 2000), p. 109.

UK national interests in taking forward the Court coincide; and that the overriding concern of the international community to bring an end to impunity for war crimes and crimes against humanity will be advanced significantly by the emergence of the ICC, with US participation. But not at any price. The US claims that the Rome Statute is flawed. Certainly, it is not perfect. While the Statute is a reflection of wide agreement which inevitably involved some compromises, none of those compromises undermines the basic fact that the Court will act only where national jurisdictions cannot.

The principal and fundamental safeguard within the Statute is the 'complementarity principle', whereby national judicial systems of states parties will have the first bite at the cherry in respect of any investigation which affects their territory or their nationals. UK courts retain the right and responsibility to investigate offences committed in the UK, or where British citizens stand accused of committing ICC crimes anywhere else in the world. The same is true in respect of the national courts of all parties, including the US if it chooses to join. The ICC will therefore be able to step in only where a national judicial system is unwilling or unable genuinely to investigate. In relation to the UK, no circumstances are foreseen under which that would apply to the British judicial system. In any case, the Prosecutor of the ICC must notify all states parties and states with jurisdiction over the case before beginning an ICC investigation, and cannot on her or his own initiative begin an investigation without first receiving the approval of a chamber of three judges. At this stage, it would be open to states to make it clear that they will themselves investigate allegations against their own nationals. In such a situation, the ICC must then suspend its investigation. The Court will only take over if the national system is unable to investigate, for example because of a breakdown in its judicial systems or because it had refused to investigate without appropriate justification. If it had investigated and subsequently refused to prosecute, the ICC could proceed only if it concluded that that decision was motivated purely by a desire to shield the individual concerned. This, it will be clear, is an unlikely prospect in the UK if an accusation appeared to have any basis in fact. And the same would undoubtedly be true in respect of the US, were an accusation to appear well founded against one of its citizens.

The UK is satisfied that its citizens enjoy the safeguards built into the Statute and is confident that UK servicemen on active duty abroad would be protected from malicious or politically motivated prosecutions. The UK has long acknowledged that the US has a lead role in defending our common values, maintaining peace and security and defending democracy and human rights throughout the world. The UK has closely aligned itself with that role and has deployed troops in different parts of the world in pursuit of those values. In 1998, the UK concluded, after the most careful consideration, that the liberty and well-being of its citizens, whether service personnel, officials, politicians or civilians, will not be threatened by malicious or politically motivated arrest and indictment in a foreign land by virtue of its commitment to the Court. With time, I hope that the US will come to share that assessment with regard to its own people, and recognise that the concerns it has expressed, legitimate as they may now seem, are not well founded.

Conclusion

It is fitting to end by returning to the overall theme of these lectures. Under the rubric of 'international criminal justice' I have had the opportunity of discussing the prospects that the ICC holds for the idea of women's justice, as well as the contribution it will make to criminal justice more generally. The ICC is part of a continuum, a process that was catalysed in Nuremberg. As regards the international aspirations of the Court, my hope is that, in years to come, there will be a broad and universal acceptance of the International Criminal

Court by all nations. The beginnings are positive; let us hope for a Court which is, in time, worthy of its name and of our continued strong support.